The Al Hound

Dennis McCarthy

John Bartholomew & Son Limited
Edinburgh and London

The Publisher wishes to thank The Kennel Club and The American Kennel Club for permission to reproduce the breed standards.

General
First published in Great Britain 1977 by
JOHN BARTHOLOMEW & SON LIMITED
12 Duncan Street, Edinburgh EH9 1TA

ISBN   0 7028 1054 1
1st edition 1977
Reprinted 1982

Prepared for the Publisher by Youé & Spooner Ltd. with illustrations by Jacqui and Malcolm Ward

Printed in Great Britain by John Bartholomew & Son Limited

Contents

Preface

It was with great pleasure that I read this book on one of the most elegant and popular breeds in the world, the Afghan Hound. All aspects of the breed are fully covered by an author whose experience in the breed has been gained over many years both as a top flight exhibitor and a worldwide judge. Some of his views are controversial but they are backed by knowledge and personal observation. In common with the other books in this series, emphasis has been placed on breed character and temperament as well as the Afghan's appearance and requirements. This will enable you to judge whether this beautiful animal is one suitable to your life style. In these pages there is something for everyone, the would-be owner, the novice and the experienced breeder.

Wendy Boorer
Consultant Editor

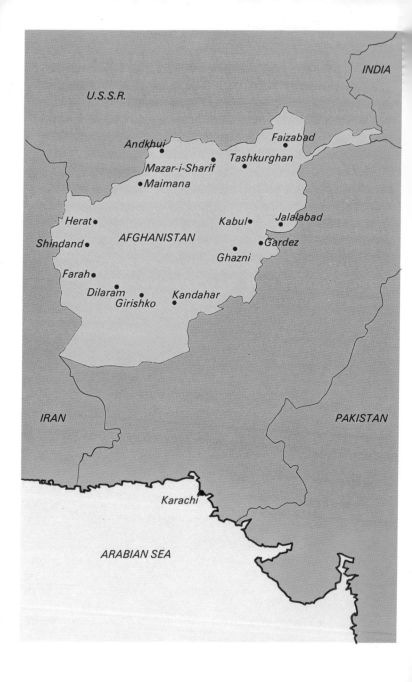

Breed history

The history of the Afghan Hound is a mixture of fact and legend, but since most Afghan owners are part romantic — why else would they let the Afghan adopt them? It would be sacrilegious to refute any of the tales handed down about the breed.

It would be difficult to go back further in time than the first legend concerning the Afghan. This claim is that this was the dog that Noah took into the Ark. Certainly the Afghan is a very *basic* dog. The true Afghan is not exaggerated in any way, so if Noah really did take one into the Ark he was choosing a dog that would give him a good start when the flood waters started to recede. But we shall never know!

The Afghan is certainly a very old breed. In 1963 there was a discovery of what is claimed to be the earliest dog. It was found in the Belt cave in Persia and dates to 9500 B.C. Even now it has not yet been studied in detail but all the preliminary reports point to it being similar in construction and conformation to the present day Greyhound group, of which we claim the Afghan to be the oldest member.

Much of the history of the Afghan, written in great detail in many books on the breed, stems from the writings of a Major Mackenzie around the end of the last century. In 1888 he was described as 'the leading authority on the breed' — but this was questionable in view of the fact that Major Mackenzie described his own dog 'Khulm' as the correct type. An observer at the time described this dog as looking like an Irish Spaniel!

Major Mackenzie was a much travelled gentleman and wrote of his journeys throughout Afghanistan. He said that Afghan Hounds are quite clearly seen in rock carvings of 'colossal size' in caves at Balkh in North East Afghanistan dating from at least 2200 B.C. Major Mackenzie also mentioned later carved inscriptions written by invaders under Alexander the Great.

Unfortunately modern explorers cannot seem to find the caves about which the Major wrote. I talked to someone who recently led an expedition to this part of Afghanistan and he told me he knew of no caves in the area or of any carvings of dogs.

Major Mackenzie is probably more reliable about recent

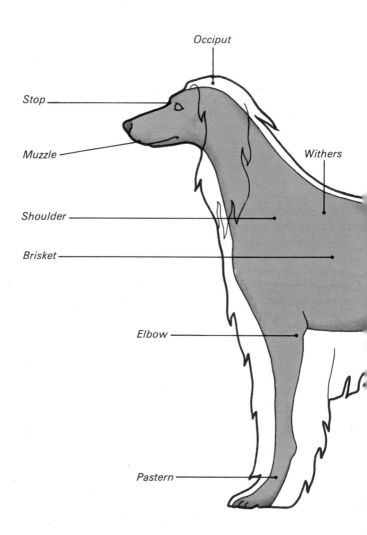

Occiput

Stop

Muzzle

Withers

Shoulder

Brisket

Elbow

Pastern

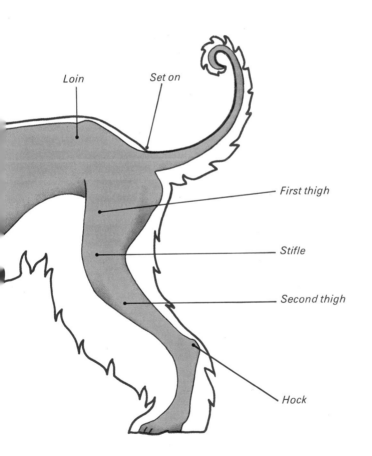

Loin

Set on

First thigh

Stifle

Second thigh

Hock

Afghan history. He kept a large number of dogs in Switzerland and around 1908 he wrote to friends in England describing his experiences in Afghanistan. I quote from one of his letters: 'The sporting dog of Afghanistan being chiefly used by the sporting Sirdars of the Royal Barukhzy family. The bitches, which are kept in seclusion by the women (as carefully guarded as mares are in Arabia) except when required to hunt, are very shy. They usually hunt in couples, bitch and dog. The bitch attacks the hinder parts and while the quarry is thus distracted, the dog, which has the great power of jaw and neck, seizes and tears the throat. Their scent, speed and endurance are remarkable, they track or run to sight equally well. Their long toes being carefully protected by tufts of hair, are serviceable on both sand and rock. Their height varies from 24 to 30in. (61 to 76cm.) Their weight from 45 to 70lb. (20 to 32kg.) Usually they are fawn or of bluish-mouse colour, but always of a darker shade on the back, which is smooth and velvety.'

I am reluctant to tear to pieces Major Mackenzie's early pre-Christian history of the Afghan. There are also reports of the Afghan's existence being mentioned on a papyrus attributed to the period 3000 to 4000 B.C., and of the Afghan being portrayed in the tombs of the Valley of the Nile. Strangely, it is said that few traces of the hound can be found in Arabia or Persia, across which the dog had to travel to get to Afghanistan, probably with the many caravans winding their way along the well worn route. In the Cairo museum there is a decorated alabaster powder bowl among the treasures of King Tutankhamen, and one scene shows hunting hounds very similar to the Afghan, but the coat is thin and sparse. One hound has leaped on the back of a leopard or gazelle, while another runs alongside. In the 1960's part of Tutankhamen's treasure was exhibited in Paris while I was attending the Paris International dog show. I searched high and low for any evidence of an Afghan living in Tut's court. I did see a ceremonial knife with what certainly appeared to have an Afghan head for a handle, but that was all.

I think we shall have to admit that there has been some fanciful writing of Afghan history in the past and it would take a lifetime of research and travel to sort out fact from fiction. But we can claim that the Afghan Hound is a very ancient breed of dog.

One of the problems in any examination of the early history

of the Afghan hound is that Afghanistan itself dates only from the mid-eighteenth century as an independent state. For 200 years before this Herat and Kandahar in the West had been in the possession of Persia, while the district of Kabul, the present capital, was included in the Mogul Empire of Delhi. Since Afghanistan's independence there have been a succession of wars involving other countries. It was the so called 'Afghan wars', towards the latter part of the last century, that introduced the Afghan Hound to Western Europe. British officers serving on these battlefronts brought back the strange looking dog to England, stolen, no doubt, from the natives, and smuggled out of the country. It was the custom for Chieftains to give an Afghan Hound to visiting dignitaries but there are many stories of how much the natives valued their bitches and would go to any length — including murder — to get them back from anyone stealing from the kennels.

The Afghan Hound has had a number of names in its time, such as the Barukhzy Hound, the Kabuli Hound, the Balkh Hound, Kurram Valley Hound and the Persian Greyhound. Many believe the last named to be the Saluki but when I did some research at the Kennel Club in London a few years ago I found a 'Persian Greyhound' entered in the Foreign Dog Class at a show in the early 1900s and two or three years later the same dog was described as an 'Afghan Hound'. I am quite sure what happened was that in that couple of years it had grown sufficient coat to become a respectable Afghan!

I firmly believe that the Afghan Hound is a purer breed than most, but there was obviously some interbreeding with similar hounds in Afghanistan. I wish I could report that the Afghan has remained pure over the centuries but in honesty I cannot. In the wild there would be no watchful kennelman to prevent interbreeding and anyone connected with dogs knows that a keen stud dog does not wait to examine the pedigree of a tempting bitch. All we can do is hope that the Afghan exercised some discretion and taste when selecting a mate!

The most famous dog of this century must be Zardin. He was shown at the Crufts dog show at Crystal Palace, London, in 1907. In the catalogue he was stated to be for sale at £525 and it is known that he was eventually sold to a firm of dealers, though his further history is not known. He won his class at that show in 1907 and he was then owned by Captain Barff. Zardin created a sensation at the show and in the press and his

Shahzada (top) and Zardin (below)

appearance was to place the Afghan high on the list of Foreign Dogs. Zardin was a full coated hound and he was commanded to present himself at the court of Queen Alexandra, wife of Edward VII. There are a number of photographs of Zardin and there is no doubt he must have impressed the court with his look of dignity and aloofness. Details are known of two litters sired by Zardin, but it is not thought that any of his progeny survived the first World War and it is doubtful if any present day Afghans are related to him.

Zardin has been fêted since that appearance in Edwardian times and he is credited with being the model for the present day breed standard the world over. But I beg to differ! Certainly he could *originally* have been the dog on which the breed standard was based. Indeed I have a copy of a letter written by Mrs. Mary Amps in 1928 in which she says: 'It is acknowledged that the finest Afghan Hound ever seen in Britain was Zardin, which was the property of Mr. Barff. He may be considered as a typical Afghan Hound. It is this type that I am exhibiting, breeding and importing into India and England. I understand that the newly formed Afghan Hound Club have taken Zardin as their standard, a wise proceeding, as it would be a pity to create a false standard for a breed popularly supposed to date back for two thousand years.'

However, a few years after this letter was written the Afghan Hound Club committee went to the British Museum to see, according to some sources, 'a portrait of Zardin to assist in formulating a new breed standard'.

For a time there was a painting of Zardin on loan to the British Museum but it was no longer there by 1930. Even so they did still have an Afghan at the Museum — a stuffed one! And I believe it was this hound that forms the basis of the breed standard world wide today.

Its name was Shahzada and it came into the Museum's possession in 1901. I have seen a letter from Mrs. Ella Whitbread of Tottenham dated February 25th, 1901. She writes: 'Do you care to have the body of my very beautiful Afghan Hound which died on Friday. The 'Shah' said he was a very beautiful specimen. I send you the enclosed to read but must beg you to send it back without fail as the friend whom is dead did the typewriting. If you will wire by return. Yours very truly, Ella Whitbread'. (There is no record of what Mrs. Whitbread enclosed with the letter). Two years later Mrs.

Whitbread offered another Afghan – Mooroo, and said 'the highest in the land had bespoken a puppy but she was never bred from'. In this later letter she referred to Shahzada and said he had been poisoned.

When I discovered that the stuffed bodies of Shahzada and Mooroo were still owned by the British Museum and stored at their depot at Tring in Hertfordshire, I wrote asking if I could borrow them to exhibit at a show I was organising. At the time I was Secretary of the Midland Afghan Hound Club. The dogs created a great deal of attention and were seen by Dr. Betsy Porter, who was a member of that Afghan committee in the early 1930's which saw the portrait of Zardin. When Dr. Porter saw the stuffed Shahzada she turned to me beaming and said: 'That's the dog we saw at the Museum. That's the dog on which we based the breed standard'. I made a note at the time (9 October 1965). Dr. Porter said that with one minor fault she thought Shahzada the perfect Afghan Hound and said I could quote her at any time.

So have we been crediting the wrong dog for the Afghan Hound breed standard? I believe so – and this is the first Afghan book to say so. I am convinced that the members of the Afghan Hound Club visiting the British Museum in the 1930's saw Shahzada. If they did have access to a stuffed Afghan and a portrait, they would take more notice of the stuffed animal. After all portrait painters are notorious for covering up warts and beautifying all that is left!

Shahzada stayed at my house for a month after the show and I had plenty of opportunity to study him carefully. I contacted the taxidermists who mounted him – they are still in business – and I was told that it is extremely difficult to present an animal *exactly* as it was when living but allowing a little for the taxidermist's licence to 'caricature' his subject, I would be happy to breed Shahzadas.

Does all this matter when considering the present day Afghan? It does, in my view. We must never lose sight of the early Afghan. Here is a natural breed, not a manufactured one. We may improve it with modern kennelling and feeding but we must never lose the characteristics that make the Afghan different from other breeds.

I have mentioned Mrs. Mary Amps. She really is responsible for the Afghan Hound we know today throughout the world. There were other importers and breeders of the Afghan but

The Afghan in the 1930s

she was to the fore. She started her kennel in Kabul where her husband was the Executive Engineer. He bought his first hound The Khan of Ghazni in 1923 as a guard for his wife, but this dog created so much excitement when they took him to Lahore that they decided to form a kennel on their return to Kabul. When she came back to England Mrs. Amps registered her Ghazni kennels and they were to become the most famous in the world. At first it was thought that Afghans would drop their coat in the English climate but after she had been back in England for about 15 months Mrs. Amps wrote that her hounds were 'without loss of feather'.

During the late 1920s and early 1930s another prominent kennel, which was to have great influence on today's Afghan, was the Bell-Murray kennel. Their hounds were much finer than the Ghazni type, more elegant, very aloof and dignified. But the Ghaznis were said by their owner to have better temperaments and were a truer type. The Ghazni/Bell-Murray controversy can still rage today and was the subject of much argument at the time. In my opinion the truth is that there are two distinct types of Afghans, a fine, sparsely coated hound living on the plain and a heavier type carrying more coat whose home was the hills. What modern breeders have done is to mix the two types but in the show ring today they are both

15

Desert or Plains hound

Mountain hound

16

evident – though the heavier Ghazni type is more popular. You could write a book on the Ghazni/Bell-Murray controversies.

The popularity of the Afghan Hound rose rapidly. The English Kennel Club officially recognised the breed in 1925 and awarded Championship status the following year. In 1926 the Afghan was introduced to America when Harpo Marx, of the Marx Brothers, imported a couple of hounds. Strangely the breed did not gain real popularity in the United States until the late thirties when some interesting imports from England gave the Afghan renewed appeal. One of its virtues was its novelty value which, coupled with its elegance, made it a natural choice for several Hollywood personalities.

The history of the Afghan must now be brought right up to date. The hound that once hunted in its native country is now bred as a companion and show dog. But never forget that this is an ancient and aristocratic hound with peculiar characteristics and temperament. It should never be bought as a novelty – this wears off all too quickly. Nor is it a dog that will settle easily into a home simply as an ornament, occupying a corner of a room and needing no care and attention.

But rather than explore its psychology, I must conclude this chapter on the history of the Afghan which turned full circle for me when I received a letter dated 13 September, 1965 from the Royal Afghan Embassy in London inquiring about the purchase of an Afghan Hound puppy from my kennel. The letter said 'we are interested mostly in hounds of a natural brown colour with long hair'.

Sadly, at that time I had no puppies for sale. . . .

The breed standard

The Breed Standard is the blueprint of the perfect dog. Each breed of dog has this standard of breed points. Some of the standards are very detailed, with precise weights and measurements, but the Afghan standard is not such a detailed one and leaves a great deal for personal preference and interpretation.

There are no proper records kept about the breed standards themselves. I have seen a report that an Afghan standard was adopted in 1912 – but if Zardin won the Foreign Dog class in 1907 one would hope there was some standard of points laid down for the judge to have any idea of the 'look' of an Afghan. There is mention in some records of an Afghan standard being registered in the late 1920s and we know that the Afghan Hound Club revised the standard in the 1930s. The English Kennel Club published their first *Standards of the Breeds* as recently as 1950. It has not been altered since then and the Afghan standard of points in almost every country of the world has been based on the English standard. I have to acknowledge the permission of the English Kennel Club to reprint their standard.

The Kennel Club Standard for the Afghan Hound

'**Characteristics** *The Afghan Hound should be dignified and aloof with a certain keen fierceness. The Eastern or Oriental expression is typical of the breed. The Afghan looks at and through one.*

General Appearance *The gait of the Afghan Hound should be smooth and springy with a style of high order. The whole appearance of the dog should give the impression of strength and dignity combining speed and power. The head must be held proudly.*

Head and Skull *Skull long, not too narrow, with prominent occiput. Foreface long with punishing jaws and slight stop. The skull well balanced and surmounted by a long topknot. Nose preferably black but liver is no fault in light coloured dogs.*

Eyes *Should be dark for preference but golden colour is not debarred. Nearly triangular, slanting slightly upwards from the inner corner to the outer.*

Ears *Set low and well back, carried close to the head. Covered* with long silky hair.

Mouth *Level.*

Neck *Long, strong with proud carriage of the head.*

Forequarters *Shoulders long and sloping, well set back, well muscled and strong without being loaded. Forelegs straight and well boned, straight with shoulder, elbows held in.*

Body *Back level, moderate length, well muscled, the back falling slightly away to the stern. Loin straight, broad and rather short. Hip bones rather prominent and wide apart. A fair spring of ribs and good depth of chest.*

Hindquarters *Powerful, well bent and well turned stifles. Great length between hip and hock with a comparatively short distance between hock and foot. The dew claws may be removed or remain, at the discretion of the breeder.*

Feet *Forefeet strong and very large both in length and breadth, and covered with long thick hair, toes arched. Pasterns long and springy, especially in front, and pads well down on the ground. Hind feet long, but not quite so broad as forefeet, covered with long thick hair.*

Tail *Not too short. Set on low with ring at the end. Raised when in action. Sparsely feathered.*

Coat *Long and very fine texture on ribs, fore and hindquarters and flanks. From the shoulder backwards and along the saddle the hair should be short and close in mature dogs. Hair long from the forehead backward, with a distinct silky topknot; on the foreface the hair is short, as on the back. Ears and legs well coated. Pasterns can be bare. Coat must be allowed to develop naturally.*

Colour *All colours are acceptable.*

Weight and Size *Ideal height: Dogs 27-29 in. (69-74cm.) Bitches 2-3 in. (5-8cm.) smaller.*

Faults *Any appearance of coarseness. Skull too wide and foreface too short. Weak underjaw. Large round or full eyes. Neck should never be too short or thick. Back too long or too short.'*

Afghan Standard, approved by the Board of Directors of the American Kennel Club, September 14th, 1948. (This has had no amendment to the time of writing).

'General Appearance *The Afghan Hound is an aristocrat, his whole appearance one of dignity and aloofness with no trace of plainness or coarseness. He has a straight front, proudly*

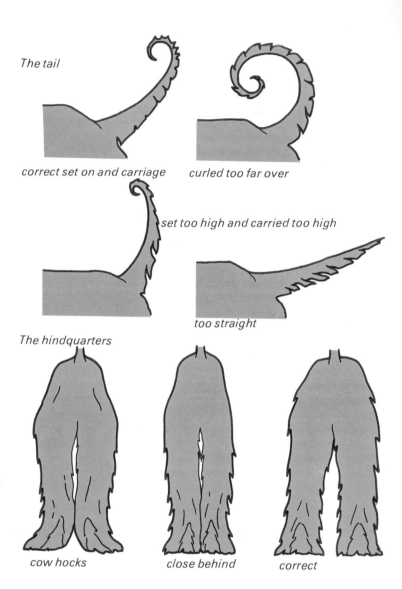

The tail

correct set on and carriage

curled too far over

set too high and carried too high

too straight

The hindquarters

cow hocks

close behind

correct

The head

Snipy with a weak muzzle

Too short in foreface

Dishface

A Borzoi head with no stop

The correct head

21

carried head, eyes gazing into the distance as if in memory of ages past. The striking characteristics of the breed – exotic, or 'Eastern' expression, long silky topknot, peculiar coat pattern, very prominent hip bones, large feet, and the impression of a somewhat exaggerated bend in the stifle due to profuse trousering – stand out clearly, giving the Afghan Hound the appearance of what he is, a King of Dogs, that has held true to tradition throughout the ages.

Head The head is of good length, showing much refinement, the skull evenly balanced with the foreface. There is a slight prominence of the nasal bone structure causing a slightly Roman appearance, the center line running up over the foreface with little or no stop, falling away in front of the eyes so there is an absolutely clear outlook with no interference; the underjaw showing great strength; the jaws long and punishing; the mouth level, meaning that the teeth from the upper jaw and lower jaw match evenly, neither overshot nor undershot. This a difficult mouth to breed. A scissors bit is even more punishing and can be more easily bred into a dog than a level mouth, and a dog having a scissors bite, where the lower teeth slip inside and rest against the teeth of the upper jaw, should not be penalised. The occipital bone is very prominent. The head is surmounted by a topknot of long silky hair.

Faults Coarseness; snipiness; overshot or undershot; eyes round or bulgy or light in color; exaggerated Roman nose; head not surmounted with topknot.

Ears The ears are long, set approximately on level with outer corners of the eyes, the leather of the ear reaching nearly to the end of the dog's nose, and covered with long silky hair.

Eyes The eyes are almond shaped (almost triangular), never full or bulgy, and are dark in color.

Nose The nose is of good size, black in color.

Neck The neck is of good length, strong and arched, running in a curve to the shoulders which are long and sloping and well laid back.

Faults Neck too short or too thick; a ewe neck; a goose neck; a neck lacking in substance.

Body The back line appearing practically level from the shoulders to the loin. Strong and powerful loin and slightly arched, falling away towards the stern, with the hip bones very pronounced; well ribbed and tucked up in the flanks. The

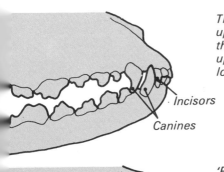

The correct 'scissors bite'. The upper incisors fit closely over the lower incisors and the upper canines fit behind the lower canines.

Incisors

Canines

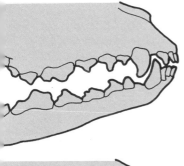

'Pincer' or 'Level bite'. Teeth of the upper jaw meet the teeth of the lower jaw.

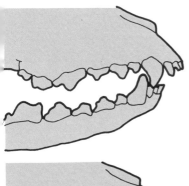

'Overshot'. The top jaw protrudes over the lower, causing a space. The canines are in reverse positions.

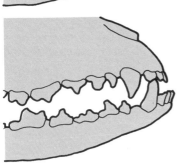

'Undershot'. The lower incisors protrude beyond the upper jaw, causing a space between the upper and lower canines.

height at the shoulders equals the distance from the chest to the buttocks; the brisket well let down, and of medium width.

Faults *Roach back, sway back, goose rump, slack loin, lack of prominence of hip bones; too much width of brisket causing interference with elbows.*

Tail *Tail set not too high on the body, having a ring, or curve on the end; should never be curled over, or rest on the back, or be carried sideways, and should never be bushy.*

Legs *Forelegs are straight and strong with great length between elbow and pastern; elbows well held in; forefeet large in both length and width; toes well arched; feet covered with long thick hair, fine in texture; pasterns long and straight; pads of feet unusually large and well down on the ground. Shoulders have plenty of angulation so that the legs are well set underneath the dog. Too much straightness of shoulder causes the dog to break down in the pasterns, and this is a serious fault. All four feet of the Afghan Hound are in line with the body, turning neither in nor out. The hind feet are broad and of good length; the toes arched, and covered with long thick hair; hindquarters powerful and well muscled, with great*

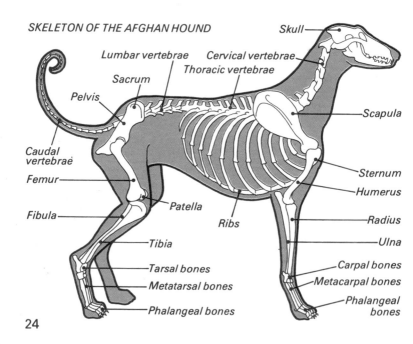

SKELETON OF THE AFGHAN HOUND

Skull

Lumbar vertebrae   Cervical vertebrae

Thoracic vertebrae

Sacrum

Pelvis

Scapula

Caudal vertebrae

Femur

Sternum

Humerus

Patella

Fibula

Ribs

Radius

Tibia

Ulna

Tarsal bones

Carpal bones

Metatarsal bones

Metacarpal bones

Phalangeal bones

Phalangeal bones

length between hip and hock; hocks are well let down; good angulation of both stifle and hock; slightly bowed from hock to crotch.

Faults *Front or back feet thrown outward or inward; pads of feet not thick enough; or feet too small; or any other evidence of weakness in the feet; weak or broken down pasterns; too straight in stifle; too long in hock.*

Coat *Hindquarters, flanks, ribs, forequarters, and legs well covered with thick, silky hair, very fine in texture; ears and all four feet well feathered; from in front of the shoulders, and also backwards from the shoulders along the saddle from the flanks and the ribs upwards, the hair is short and close, forming a smooth back in mature dogs – this is a traditional characteristic of the Afghan Hound. The Afghan Hound should be shown in its natural state; the coat is not clipped or trimmed; the head is surmounted (in the full sense of the word) with a topknot of long, silky hair – this is also an outstanding characteristic of the Afghan Hound. Showing of short hair on cuffs on either front or back legs is permissible.*

Faults *Lack of short haired saddle in mature dogs.*

Height *Dogs; 27 inches, plus or minus one inch. Bitches; 25 inches, plus or minus one inch.*

Weight *Dogs; about 60 pounds. Bitches; about 50 pounds.*

Color *All colors are permissible, but color or color combinations are pleasing; white markings, especially on the head, are undesirable.*

Gait *When running free, the Afghan Hound moves at a gallop, showing great elasticity and spring in his smooth, powerful stride. When on a loose lead, the Afghan can trot at a fast pace; stepping along, he has the appearance of placing the hind feet directly in the foot prints of the front feet, both thrown straight ahead. Moving with head and tail high, the whole appearance of the Afghan Hound is one of great style and beauty.*

Temperament *Aloof and dignified, yet gay.*

Faults *Sharpness or shyness.'*

It is quite obvious that both the American and English standards combine the two 'types' of Afghans, and it says a good deal for the Afghan Clubs who agreed on the standard of points. Afghan Clubs the world over have been notorious in being unable to agree on so many aspects of Afghans. In Britain most breeds of dog have a Breed Council formed of the different Clubs within a breed to get conformity of judging lists

International Champion Tzara of Pooghan
Champion Tara of Pooghan
and Champion Zaza of Khorrassan
Three beautiful bitches happily living together, showing glamour,
personality and good temperament

International and Scandinavian Champion
Eduardo del Flamante
The author made this dog Best in Show at a dog show in Sweden

Champion Horningsea Tigers Eye, a brindle

Head study of Pooghans Cassius whose pedigree blends Dutch and English breeding 27

and recommendations to the Kennel Club. There have been a dozen attempts to run an Afghan Breed Council but all have failed after a few months. There is so much controversy surrounding the Afghan that we should congratulate and appreciate the Afghan enthusiasts who were able to agree one standard of points.

If there is ever any discussion about the Afghan breed standard it must be appreciated that a personal view is being expressed, but it is interesting to compare the American and British standards, remembering that we are all trying to breed the same dog.

The gait described in the British standard is really of very little help to the judge and I would like to see a full and proper description of movement detailed. The head is a problem to describe – and also to breed! In the early 1970s judges seemed to favour a fine head with a narrow jaw. This was totally improper, in my view. I look at an Afghan head and expect it to denote the sex of the dog. A bitch's head is feminine and a dog's head is masculine. Remember that writing of 70 odd years ago which stated 'the dog has the great power of jaw to seize and tear his quarry's throat'.

Ignore the 'level' bite mentioned in the standards. I have judged over 2,000 dogs in Europe and Scandinavia and I have only seen half a dozen Afghans with a level bite. A 'scissor' bite with the upper jaw fitting firmly over the lower is the real 'bite' of an Afghan. The British allow the liver coloured nose in lighter dogs. This is so common world wide that I would have thought the Americans would have allowed it. The Americans call for eyes 'dark in colour' – the British allow a 'golden' eye – but I have actually known judges stating a preference for a 'light eye' as being a 'far seeing eye'. This is nonsense. The light eye in an Afghan is a fault. It is offensive and detracts greatly from the expression of the animal.

The ears are better described in the American standard as to their setting but I doubt that nature ever intended the length of the nose to be a yardstick for the length of the ears!

The Afghan's shoulder is vaguely described in both standards. I think this should be more definite and I look for an ideal shoulder angulation of 45° when I judge. A shoulder that is too upright will produce an improper movement in front, and this should be listed as a fault.

A level topline in an Afghan is certainly a desirable feature but the length of back often causes argument. I have known judges highly praise a 'short-coupled' Afghan. Short-coupling might be highly desired in some breeds but the Afghan must move quickly and soundly and a really short back would impede its progress. The ring tail is a desired characteristic and I am surprised that neither standard penalises the straight tail. They should do.

The Afghan's coat is a matter of some controversy still – the 'silky coat' is rarely seen today and a woollier coat is common, but I agree wholeheartedly with the Americans who frown on a clipped or trimmed coat. The coat *must* be allowed to develop naturally – and that means no scissoring or razoring to 'improve' the shape of the dog. The 'saddle' has been a sore point with many breeders and there was talk at one time of removing from the British standard the mention of the short hair on the back of the dog forming a 'saddle'. The phrase 'in a mature dog' is a let out. Most Afghans don't mature until they're 7 or 8 years old – so should we penalise the absence of a saddle in a younger dog?

The truth about the Afghan's coat is that we have in a sense 'created' this ourselves. You would not dream of using a sparsely coated dog at stud. The well coated dogs get all the stud work that's going – so by selection we have now bred a heavily coated dog, and this has inevitably meant the saddle has disappeared. To satisfy everyone – leave the wording in the standard concerning the saddle as it is – and for further explanation use the excuse that a saddle comes along with the mature dog. By the time your dog is 'mature' it will have long left the show ring due to old age!

If you get your Afghan to stand up and go over him reading the breed standard at the same time you might be dispirited or elated – depending on your interpretation of the standard. But breed standards disintegrate when you realise the truth of the old doggy saying – 'The perfect dog has yet to be born'. All we can do is strive for the best. Keep a watchful eye on the standard and aim to get a dog that can be lived with. It is interesting that the British standard does not mention temperament, the most important characteristic of any dog. A well known judge once wrote that a true Afghan should have balance and rhythm. This cuts the breed standards down to a simple phrase that ought to be remembered by every judge and breeder of an Afghan Hound.

Choosing a puppy

Choosing an Afghan Hound puppy for pet or show is a very difficult task, particularly when it is very young. When I first started in dogs I took a keen interest in seeing as many different breeds of puppies as possible. I looked at Shih Tzus, Irish Setters, Cocker Spaniels, Beagles, Boxers, Borzois, Poodles, Basset Hounds, Fox Terriers, and many more. And after examining all the different breeds of puppies in the nest I can honestly say that assessing an Afghan's potential is the most difficult.

In nearly every other breed there is some characteristic, some peculiarity that will give a clue as to the identity of the breed, and there is also evidence of faults and virtues. But not with the Afghan puppy. If you look at an adult Afghan and then look at a young puppy, you will begin to appreciate the difficulty. The adult has shape, coat, size — the puppy has none of these things and quite honestly you have to take the breeder's word that it is a pedigree Afghan!

But, since a choice has to be made, let us examine what to look for, and what to avoid.

First, condition yourself to buying a puppy. Ask yourself why you want an Afghan. Is it just that it is a novelty, a fashionable dog to own? These are not good reasons. Have you the time to care properly for an Afghan pup? If you are out at work all day, think again. If you live in a flat, then an Afghan is not for you. A puppy Afghan must have regular meals, and takes time to house train, and to groom when the coat starts growing. It will need exercising. Do you still want an Afghan?

I cannot emphasise too strongly the importance of buying an Afghan from a recognised breeder. Avoid kennels that deal in all breeds of dogs. These dealing kennels may serve a purpose in supplying some breeds of puppies but the Afghan Hound is not the dog to be sold like a washing machine or any other piece of merchandise. You may need assistance with a problem and you must buy from someone with practical knowledge of the breed.

You can find a breeder by writing to the Kennel Club, who will be happy to supply a list of people who breed Afghans. But, remember, by supplying this list they are not necessarily *recommending* the breeders. You can also find a breeder by attending dog shows. This is a very good way because here

Four-day-old whelps

you will be able to see stock from the breeder's kennel, and at the larger dog shows, where a number of Afghans may be exhibited, you will be able to find out who has puppies available. Puppies are also advertised in the dog papers. But do choose a reputable breeder. I could tell so many stories of dealing kennels concerning poor stock, false pedigrees and sometimes false pretences. I found out that one kennel of dog dealers was giving *MY* name and address when they sold an Afghan Hound, telling their customers that I would sort out any problems! The stock they were selling had nothing at all to do with me or my breeding!

When you find out which breeder has puppies available, make a proper appointment and make sure too that you have not been in contact with any dogs that have been ill. Go armed with as many questions as possible.

If you want a puppy as a pet you are really only concerned with one point – temperament. Sadly this was neglected for many years and the result was that many bad tempered Afghans were bred, but the situation has changed now.

You are really looking for a bold, healthy, happy puppy, whether for pet or show. When we get an inquiry for a puppy we usually like the prospective owner to see the puppies at three to four weeks and, if he is happy with what he sees in our kennel, he can collect the puppy at eight weeks of age. As I have already said, the breed points of the baby Afghan at four weeks are just not there, so ask to see the parents of the puppy. If you like the look of the parents then the chances are you will like your puppy. The opposite applies, of course, for if you do not like the parents you will almost certainly be disappointed in the puppy later.

You must forgive the puppy's mother for a lack of coat. Some mothers drop nearly all their coat when they have puppies, and what coat they keep gets tangled badly, so do not expect the dam to be in top show condition. But she should have a good temperament. She may not welcome you if her babies are very young, but, if her puppies are eight weeks old, then she should not show disapproval if you handle them.

Ask to see the sire of the puppies if he is in the kennel. This may not be possible because he may belong to another kennel but if there is a chance of seeing him, try and do so. In a larger kennel you may be able to see several generations of Afghans all relating to the puppies.

Before you actually visit the kennel make up your mind whether you want a dog or bitch and make up your mind about colour. In the show ring colour doesn't matter – all colours are acceptable. But if you have a preference for a certain colour tell the breeder before you visit the kennel. It is a waste of time to visit a kennel to look at all the puppies – you will be lost for choice and this wastes everyone's time.

You must make allowances if the puppy is shy for the first few minutes. If it lives outside the house then the inside may be strange to it. The aloof dignity is an *adult* characteristic – a puppy should be bold and friendly. After a few minutes the puppy should come towards you openly, tail wagging. If the puppy is cringing and obviously terrified of you, don't buy it. And a bad tempered puppy is to be avoided at all costs. The temperament of the puppy is all important. The temperament of the Afghan parents is important too but they may well be more suspicious of you than the puppy is. They should be reasonably friendly toward you or again they may ignore you altogether.

A puppy at eight weeks

If the puppy is about eight weeks of age it will play with its mother but its father will treat it disdainfully — at least when *YOU* are watching.

Choosing an Afghan puppy for the show ring is almost impossible. There can be no guarantee of any of the desired show points developing. It is a matter of breeding, pedigree, rearing, developing and most of all, *LUCK!*

At eight weeks of age you would not expect the head shape to be perfect, though a coarse head — that is a wide head with no length of nose might be apparent. There is no way that you can assess coat but a look at the parents might be helpful here. In the show ring a fairly big Afghan is preferred and I believe that we are now breeding Afghans an inch or two above the natural size, but remember the final size of the adult dog depends to a great extent on sensible rearing from the weaning stage.

Obviously you want a healthy puppy. There should be no discharge from the eyes or nose. What little coat the puppy has should be soft and slightly glossy. You should be suspicious if the puppy scratches a great deal. If you want a show specimen avoid a puppy with a third eyelid: this is a membrane of skin in the corner of an eye. This does not matter in the pet Afghan and, in any case, I have known this third eyelid to disappear with maturity.

Try to avoid a skinny puppy – the body should be nice and firm, and the leg bones should be strong. The hind leg angulation so desired in the show ring is not always present in a puppy – this can develop later. The ring tail will almost certainly not show on a young puppy and may not develop for several months.

Eight weeks of age is a good time to buy a puppy and it will be ready for its new home. But do not be put off because a puppy is older. The twelve-week-old youngster is starting to develop more characteristics and could be a better buy. On the other hand the bolder and more attractive puppies might go first from a litter, so once you have made up your mind about a puppy do not delay in buying it. Do not buy a puppy under the age of eight weeks.

Some more points to watch for. In a male dog make sure you can feel two testicles. It is rare for an Afghan to have problems in this direction. A bad mouth in an Afghan is also a rarity. Examine the mouth. The upper jaw should fit just over the underjaw. If there is a problem with teeth, the breeder should be honest with you about this. Eye shape is difficult to assess but, in a show specimen, large round eyes are not desirable. The ear set can usually be seen in a puppy. The ears should start on a level with the eyeline. The tail set and carriage is a problem but if you do want a puppy for show avoid a tail that is looped right over the back.

Be suspicious of any breeder advertising 'show puppies for sale'. I hope I have convinced you by now that there is no such thing as a 'show puppy'. British breeders were horrified to read several years ago in an American dog magazine – 'Puppies for sale. Guaranteed in writing to finish Champions'. Later I learned that American breeders had been just as horrified.

34

Be wary of the breeder who enthuses about the ownership of one of his or her puppies without pointing out the drawbacks and problems. And be very suspicious of promises about an Afghan puppy's development. When we sell a puppy from our kennel we take at least an hour to point out the pitfalls as well as the pleasures of owning an Afghan. We inquire fully about accommodation and exercise facilities and about the time that a prospective owner has to spend with the puppy. We make no promises as to a puppy's potential in the show ring. We aim to sell a sound, bold, healthy, happy puppy and we guarantee the pedigree. If there was a definite show fault we would advise accordingly. Anyone selling a puppy in a different way from this is doing no service to you, himself, the breed or the dog.

How I wish I could accurately describe the correct size, weight, and shape of a puppy, but they vary in these things. You choose by instinct and, if a correct choice is made, another Afghan Champion is added to the kennel. But in Afghan Hounds I have to tell you, sadly, that most puppies just don't work out, and while you may have a happy companion, it really is quite likely to be a mutt as far as the show ring is concerned! Potential is almost impossible to assess. I have seen the runt of a litter – much smaller than the rest – grow up into a full size beautiful Afghan, and I have seen the pick of the litter turn out to be an undersized adult. I have seen two straight tailed parents produce offspring with lovely ring tails. I have seen two sparsely coated Afghans produce full coated children. Many a Champion has parents that you wouldn't look twice at. And, sadly, many a very ordinary Afghan has parents – both Champions – who would not wish to acknowledge that they had produced such a mundane specimen.

When choosing a pet for a companion you can forgive that third eyelid, or the straight tail carried right over the back, or the poor angulation or the sparse coat, or the thick head. The Afghan with all these faults can be a great pal with the right temperament. But in the show ring these faults are totally unacceptable and, unfortunately, they can and do sometimes develop in the most promising puppy.

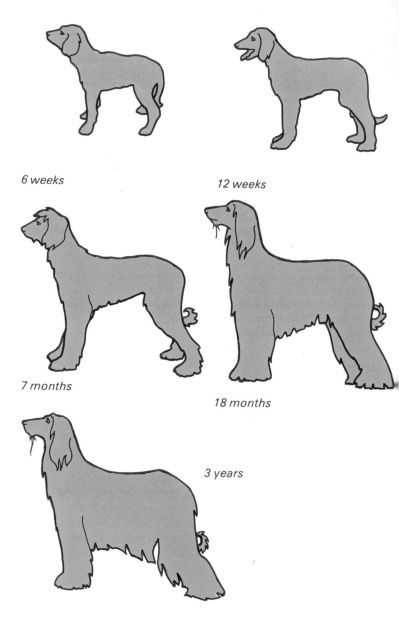

6 weeks

12 weeks

7 months

18 months

3 years

Typical stages in the growth and development of the Afghan

General care

Feeding

The Afghan puppy must be fed regularly and well. The desirable Afghan today is a big dog with a firm body and strong bone, and you will only get this with good and proper feeding. I do not agree with breeders who issue charts with weights to be attained by a certain age. Afghans differ so much that these guides are a waste of time in practical terms and cause concern if the puppies go over or under the 'recommended' weight. When we sell a puppy we give a diet sheet. It is simple and sensible but it has to be followed closely.

> 5 meals a day until 3 months old
> 4 meals a day from 3-5 months
> 3 meals a day from 5-8 months
> 2 meals a day from 8-12 months
> After this one main meal daily

The meals consist of two milky feeds a day of warmed milk, a raw egg added and thickened with high quality baby cereal powder. A puppy should have two cooked meat meals daily, mixed with good quality graded puppy meal. Good quality canned dog meat can be used for these meals if more convenient. And there should be one meal a day of fresh raw meat.

Canovel tablets (available from your vet) should be given and most puppies will readily accept these as a 'treat'. These are multi vitamin and mineral tablets and will probably make up for anything missing from the regular meals. Bone flour is a useful addition to meaty meals and your vet will advise about getting a flour that is easily assimilated.

Fresh water should be available at all times, and it is best to feed at regular times and take up any uneaten food. For a young puppy marrow bones will strengthen teeth development – but never smaller bones which can do an enormous amount of damage internally. Never give chicken or rabbit bones.

Porridge can be used occasionally for a milky feed, just to vary the diet a little, and boiled fish (boned) will be beneficial.

It is very difficult to stipulate set amounts of food. Generally the Afghan is a sensible eater and will take sufficient for its needs. Put plenty of food down and your puppy will indicate when it has had enough. It is quite a good idea to have a small bowl of good quality dog biscuits available. The puppy will want to exercise its teeth on these and this eases wear and tear on slippers, shoes and chair legs.

When you collect your puppy from the breeder it will probably have been wormed twice, but it is usually advisable to worm again at about four months of age.

I cannot over stress the importance of feeding puppies good quality food. There are plenty of cheap canned meats and biscuit meals but these have little food value, and often cause upset digestive systems, and they are a waste of money with young puppies. Puppies up to the age of six months rarely eat more than is good for them but after this they can get overweight. As a general guide to proper weight the hip bones should always show. If they are covered it is a sign that the dog is overweight, and this should be avoided. The Afghan generally is a lean looking hound and, while you do not want ribs showing and making the dog look as though it is suffering from malnutrition, you do not want a fat Afghan because this can bring a number of problems later.

The use and source of minerals and vitamins is quite a complicated subject and there is still a great amount of research to be done in this field. But to simplify the matter these are the six main vitamins, A, B, C, D, E, and K, and there are many subdivisions of these.

This may seem complicated and a little frightening if you think you have to assess and balance every particle of food to ensure that the dog is getting a balanced vitamin intake in his diet, but in practice, of course, it doesn't work out like that. There is no point in searching four or five times a day for all the vitamin requirements of an Afghan, because good food contains everything the puppy and adult Afghan needs to grow into a healthy dog.

The mineral requirement seems almost as complicated as the vitamin needs, but only minute amounts are needed, and these are all present in good food. For example, calcium for teeth and bones, phosphorus for growth. Protein is an important part of a dog's diet – milk, meat, eggs and cheese are the main sources.

Frankly, to go into more detail about vitamins, minerals and proteins is unnecessary in practical terms. Sensible feeding will prevent the host of dietary deficiency problems that can

Vitamin:	Bodily Function of Vitamin:	Source of Vitamin:
A	Assists with vision, healthy skin growth and reproduction, and prevention of infection	Most animal fats, fish liver oils, butter, cream, cheese and egg yolk
B	Oxidation processes and proper absorption of food. Vital for sustained growth and good appetite. Aids regular bowel movements	Yeast, liver, milk, egg yolk
C	Proper absorption of some foods but not normally essential in dog diet as adult dogs manufacture their own	Liver, green leaves and fruit
D	Assists growth, reproduction, etc., by helping intestinal absorption of calcium for strong bones	Cod liver oil and other fish liver oils
E	Helps build body tissue. Aids reproductive process and believed to help bitches in milk	Wheatgerm, soya bean, vegetable oils, whole cereal grains
K	Controls clotting of blood and assists with some basic body processes	Fresh green leaves, liver, egg, etc.

occur, but rarely do.

Most Afghans gain full size at fourteen to eighteen months, and when this is reached the job of feeding is much easier. The Afghan will be content with almost any kind of food and, if you aim for a varied, interesting diet, your dog will be content and healthy. There is no need for your dog's diet to be any less interesting than your own. Our adult Afghans get fresh raw

At thirteen months of age

meat, eggs, fish, wholemeal biscuits, canned dog food, tripe and a dry 'complete' dog biscuit.

You are not doing your dog a favour if you feed it an exclusive diet of best steak and chicken.

Some Afghan breeders feed a 'natural' diet of meat and herbs. Personally I am not in favour of puppies being reared on a natural diet because the chances are the new owner will want to feed in a more conventional way. There are some interesting books on natural feeding but it is unfair to foist your own practice on others and I would suggest thorough research into the subject before accepting any natural feeding and rearing method with your own dog.

I am not against the feeding of table scraps to the adult Afghan and variation of diet is, I think, important. Many breeders recommend one day a week fasting, with no food available but plenty of fresh drinking water. We occasionally practise this at our kennel and it certainly does no harm. If your Afghan does get overweight, you must ration the food supply. If there is no medical reason for too much weight it is almost certainly too much food and, perhaps, too little exercise.

For all their elegance and breeding Afghans are not able to keep their ears out of the feeding bowl, and it is a good idea to protect them at meal times. You can start from puppyhood by fitting a 'snood', which is simply a cut off stocking top that holds the ears close to the head and prevents them dropping into the food.

Feeding dish and Afghan with snood

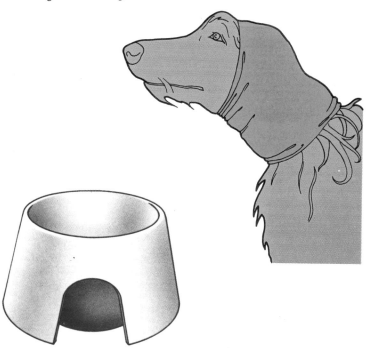

If ever you see worms in your Afghan's motions have a veterinary check up, and you might consider anyway worming your dog regularly – say once every two months.

You must, of course, vaccinate your puppy against distemper and leptospirosis. Most vets vaccinate at twelve weeks and again at fourteen weeks. On no account should a puppy that has not been vaccinated mix with other dogs or frequent any place where dogs are known to have visited. The vaccination causes no problems nowadays and your youngster will not be off its food or suffer any other visible effect. Do not take any notice of any advice you might be told or read that vaccination is unnecessary and that constant attention to hygiene is sufficient.

Vaccinate at twelve weeks and be advised by your vet as to booster injections if you really care for your puppy's life.

Housing
If you intend keeping just one or two Afghans, you will probably want them as companions in the house because they make excellent house pets. They are fairly easy to house train and, if the temperament is right, they are affectionate toward children and to the immediate family, and they will tolerate strangers. But you must always remember that the Afghan is a hunting breed and care must be taken that it is secure and cannot get out into the streets or open country.

One question we ask of a potential owner is: 'Have you got a garden and is it well fenced?' Before you purchase your puppy make sure it has a good area for exercise. Fences and hedges should be checked carefully for any escape routes.

If you are going to house your Afghan outside, a large kennel is needed with sleeping quarters that are tall enough for the *adult* Afghan to stand up, with at least six to nine inches clearance over the head, and room for the Afghan easily to turn around. We are really talking of a kennel 5ft. 6in. (1.65m.) in length; 4ft (1.20m.) high; and 4ft. (1.20m.) wide. With an outside kennel a chain-link fenced exercise area of at least 6yds. (5.52m.) by 3yds. (2.76m.) is required. But remember, living in this confined area would be a dull existence for the dog, so walking on a lead and a good gallop in a *very* secure and escape-proof field would ensure contentment.

Never bed your Afghan on hay or straw. It gets into the coat and creates matting which is very uncomfortable for the dog.

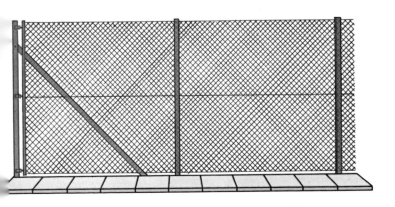

Chain link and steel supports

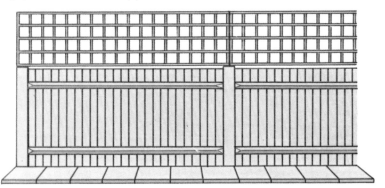

The paving stones prevent the dog from digging its way out

Suitable methods of fencing for confining the Afghan

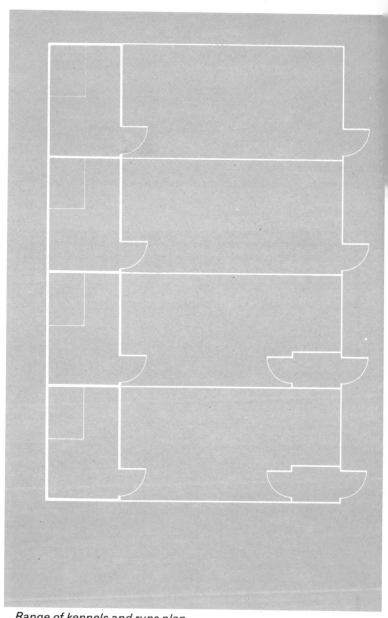

Range of kennels and runs plan

A single kennel unit outside

Shredded paper makes good bedding material, but your pet will prefer an old coat or pullover although this can harbour undesirable parasites. It is a good idea to get your Afghan a sleeping box whether it is going to live inside or outside in a kennel. But do not be influenced by the size of your puppy – get a box large enough for an adult dog. I would recommend buying a fibre glass bed measuring 40in. (1.00m.) by 24in. (60cm.). Do not buy a wooden or basket bed. This soon begins to lose its shape and strength when the puppy's teeth get to work.

Exercise

Exercising an Afghan is something of a problem. There is nothing an Afghan enjoys more than a really good run, but you have a hound that unfortunately will rarely obey any command when running free. If you do let your Afghan loose, make sure you are well away from any traffic. Try to find a field with a closely knit hedge, and make sure there are no sheep or cattle around. It can be very embarrassing if you let your Afghan out of your sight and it returns herding a flock of sheep! It has happened many times but farmers are not likely to be as amused as you may be.

It is a great sight to see Afghans running free but be warned that they can travel very fast and go some distance before they tire. They will usually return – but in their own time. The safest form of exercise is, of course, on a lead. Make sure this is a slip lead with no chance of the dog escaping from it. Many cities have by-laws insisting that all dogs should have the name and address of the owner clearly imprinted or attached to a collar. Unfortunately Afghans do not take too kindly to collars and they mark the coat around the neck in a way that would be noticeable in the show ring, though perhaps this is not so important in the pet dog. Our own hounds are restricted in a large compound and are safe from escape, so they do not need to wear collars. You can leave your dog collarless only if there is no chance for it to escape.

The Afghan usually enjoys a walk on a lead and you should get it used to this at an early age, as soon as the vaccination is effective. A brisk walk should be attempted between lamp posts. Be sensible about your dog doing its toilet in the street. Fouling of footpaths is usually an offence and your neighbours will hardly tolerate this nuisance. I am not going to lay down here any rigid rule about the amount of exercise an Afghan requires. It would be improper to say 'at least two miles a day' because I know healthy, happy Afghans that do not walk two miles a month! Many Afghans are content to lie all day on a comfortable settee, but it is obviously not a healthy life and will promote slack muscles and general lack of fitness.

Do watch your puppy when it exercises. You cannot wrap it up in a cocoon, but a puppy needs watching so that it does not go too wild and injure itself.

Adult Afghans sometimes have to be urged to take a walk but once they are exercising they are happy, and they really enjoy going out with their owners. The Afghan is an extrovert and enjoys attention at all times despite that dignified and aloof appearance.

Basic Training

The Afghan is a very independent dog. Critics say this is a drawback; enthusiasts say this is part of the charm of the breed. You will meet Afghan owners who declare that the dog is 'untrainable', but this is not necessarily so. You *can* get a

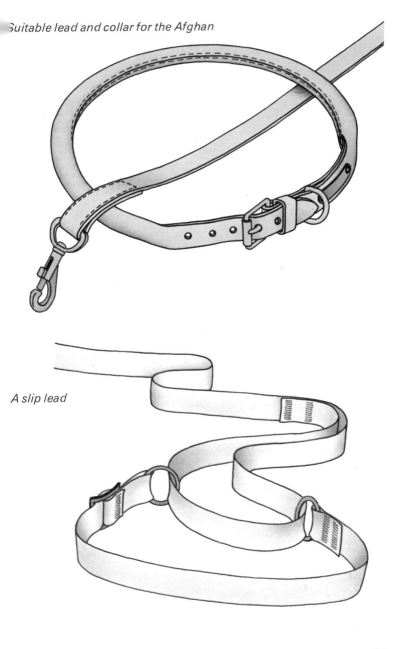

A slip lead

good degree of obedience with some care and time and thought.

As a puppy in the nest he is probably used to sleeping and playing with his litter brothers and sisters and now he is to spend his first night alone. So you begin your Afghan training as soon as the puppy arrives at his new home. As soon as he is aware of his surroundings, play with him and keep him active. Do *not* let him go to sleep on that first evening home until *you* are ready to retire for the night. The Afghan's box should be ready for him and if it is cold wrap up a hot water bottle and put it in the box. An article of clothing in the box is a good idea too. The smell of a human's clothes seems to be comforting to a young puppy. I have also known a loud ticking clock in the puppy's box to act as a calming influence. You must be prepared to see to the puppy perhaps a couple of times during the first two or three nights at home. If he wakes in the middle of the night, he may be bewildered by finding himself in strange surroundings. Do *not* take him into your bedroom unless you want an extra sleeping companion for life! There is no point in actually hitting the puppy that howls in the middle of the night. Persuade him by the *tone* in your voice that he had better go back to his box – or else!

House training is important. The Afghan grows into a *BIG* dog and it is capable of flooding a large area! As soon as the puppy has had a meal put it outside to do its toilet. It is a natural sequence of events that as it fills itself with food it will empty itself afterwards. Keep an eye on the puppy outside to make sure he has performed before coming back into the house. Most Afghans are anxious to be clean in their habits but some perseverance is sometimes necessary to get your hound house trained.

Put clean newspaper down near the door. When the puppy makes for the exit – that's the signal – quickly open the door. Your speed determines the number of 'accidents' in the house!

A puppy making a toilet mistake in the house must be disciplined. A sharp word – 'No! Naughty' will get him out of the habit.

Your Afghan will probably have a grand sounding pedigree name but you may have to find a more suitable name for him for every day use. As soon as the name is selected, get him used to it by calling him as much as possible. The more time you are able to spend with your puppy, the more obedient he will become. And all the time discipline is very important. It is useless putting off discipline 'because he's only a puppy'. You are going to have a big dog, and a big disobedient dog is a pleasure to no one. Start your discipline early. Scolding in a sharp tone is the best method. Never, *never* use a rolled up newspaper to threaten your Afghan. You will soon have a cringing dog that you could never proudly show visitors, or judges in the show ring. A hard smack is to be avoided, but tapping on the nose is acceptable, especially if your puppy starts to bite which it may well do in play. This is a bad habit and should be stopped immediately.

Personally I am very much against the Afghan being trained as a guard dog. As recently as a hundred years ago this hound was sometimes quite savage. It probably had to be to survive. This has been bred out of the dog, but the spark may still be there and I am convinced that the really bad tempered Afghan that one occasionally sees in the street and in the showring is the result of improper discipline.

Think about joining your local dog training club. There is probably one near you that meets regularly. The Kennel Club will be pleased to send you details of such a club. Unfortunately Afghans have quite a reputation for being difficult dogs to train but a high degree of obedience *is* obtainable and training classes can be of help. In America Afghans have been seen in the obedience ring and I have even heard of an Obedience Champion. In England, I must tell you that I have not heard of one successful Afghan at obedience shows. But when you feel like giving up the training programme just remember that, a few years ago in Leicester, a blind person used an Afghan as a guide dog.

It is against the nature of the breed to be a super obedient dog and, if you want such an animal, an Afghan is not for you. But the Afghan is a very intelligent creature anxious to please its owner. I am sure the secret of successful living with an Afghan is affection. And it is a two way deal. Any affection you show to the dog will be repaid in full.

Grooming

A clean, well groomed Afghan is a delight to the eye and a pleasure to own. A dirty, matted one is usually a miserable specimen and is mostly hidden from sight. An Afghan needs more attention to coat than any other breed and you must realise this before buying one. On the other hand most doggy people will admit that an Afghan in full bloom is the most handsome and glamorous dog in the canine world.

The Afghan puppy has very little coat and it is amusing to see prospective owners expecting a puppy to be a miniature Afghan with a few inches of coat nearly hanging to the ground. There is no appreciable amount of coat until five months or so. But from eight weeks the Afghan puppy can be bathed as it gets him used to the treatment he can expect later. But fast and efficient drying is important when bathing a puppy.

From eight to twelve months the growth of coat is very noticeable, and it needs regular attention to keep it well groomed. It is at the end of this period that the coat changes. The puppy coat 'drops' and the adult coat starts growing through. The Afghan's coat does not come loose, like a Labrador or Alsatian, and you will not find hairs all over the furniture. When the coat is changing from puppy to adult it does tend to mat, but regular and correct grooming will prevent this.

It is not necessary to groom every day – and if this is done you will certainly remove more coat than is grown and you will have a bald Afghan in no time! Your Afghan needs a *thorough* grooming at least once a week. And 'thorough' is the all important word. Check all over to see if there are any mats. If there are, loosen these by hand. Do not use a comb, it will be too painful. Brush your Afghan's coat *from the roots* working on a small area at one time. Do not 'surface' brush – you will not get down to the roots and mats will form which can be painful and result in sores developing. On your weekly grooming you should not take out more than a brushful of coat. Don't be too fierce with your brushing. The aim is to keep as much coat as possible on the dog.

You can use talcum powder to clean and freshen your Afghan but this must be used sparingly and, again, thorough grooming from the roots of the coat is essential. Pay particular attention round the ears, where mats form easily, and in the

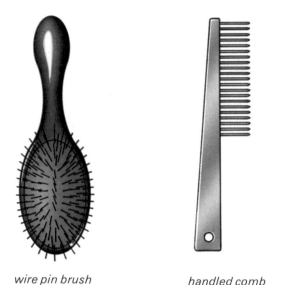

wire pin brush   *handled comb*   *wide tooth comb*

Grooming tools

table model dryer, with flexible tube extension

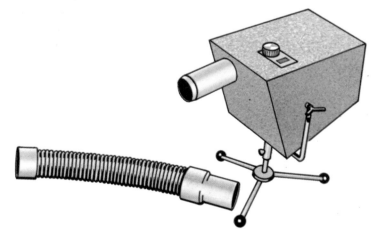

groin. Use a wire-pin brush for your first grooming and after this you can use a wide tooth comb. Do not use a 'tangle comb' or 'knot remover' or claw brush. These gadgets are too severe for the Afghan and will remove far too much coat. If the Afghan gets very dirty you may have to forgo some of the brushing before bathing because the coat may be brittle and again you will start to rip it.

It may surprise you to know that there is some controversy about grooming and a few years ago a bitter argument developed in England when a well known breeder wrote an article in a Club magazine on the grooming of Afghans. I will tell you how we groom and bath in our kennel and it is up to you whether you follow our method.

We groom first and then bathe. The amount of pre-bath grooming does depend on the condition of the coat. Stand your Afghan in a large sink or bath and use a hose or spray from the tap. Make sure that the water is neither too hot nor too cold, and soak the dog thoroughly, making sure the water penetrates the coat. There are no half measures to bathing an Afghan. Do it properly or wait until you have enough time to devote to the job. Just damping the Afghan does no good at all. Don't allow the dirty water to fill the bath or sink. Soak the Afghan with warm water making sure the water is draining away all the time. Then shampoo the dog thoroughly. We often use a coconut oil shampoo. It leaves a pleasing gloss on the coat without clogging it with oil or grease, but there are some excellent shampoos on the market and you can use a basic dog shampoo if you like. Every other bath we use a coat conditioner to put back into the coat the natural oils removed when the dog is bathed.

Never use a soap or detergent. These will irritate the skin and almost certainly create a host of skin problems. Use good quality shampoo and rub and massage well through to the roots all over the dog. Be very careful of the eyes and inside the ears. Try to avoid these areas when working up a lather. The Afghan then needs rinsing thoroughly making sure all the shampoo is removed. When rinsed, shampoo all over again right through to the roots, working up a good lather that should be clean this time. All the dirt should have been removed with that first bath. Then the final rinsing, and I must emphasise again that all the shampoo must be removed from the coat. Start rinsing from the head, taking care round the

Bathing and grooming sequence

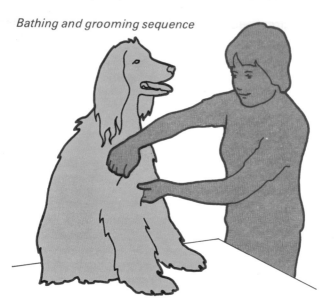

1. De-tangling. Pulling apart mats and tangles

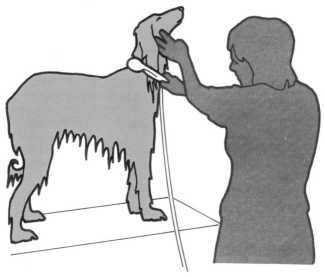

2. Wetting thoroughly with hair spray or similar, at start of bathing operation

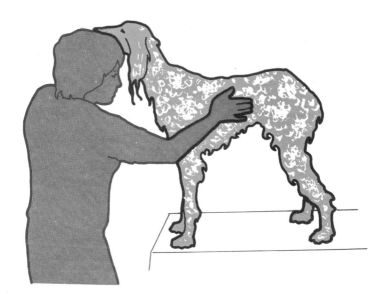

3. Soaping thoroughly with good quality shampoo

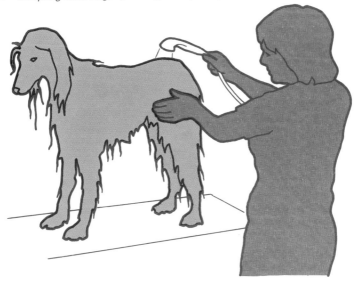

4. Rinsing thoroughly (with hair spray) all shampoo out of coat

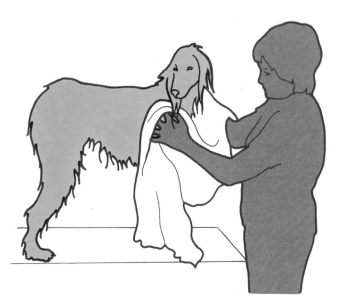

5.   *Towelling briskly and thoroughly after final rinse*

6.   *Drying and brushing-deep from the roots of the coat*

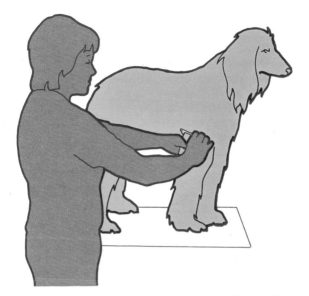

7. *After the brushing – combing through (with wide-tooth comb)*

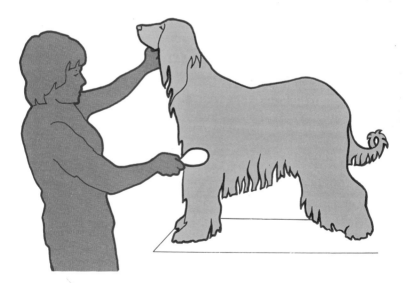

8. *The final brushing and finished Afghan*

eyes and ears, then down the neck, along the body and down each leg, squeezing and rinsing all the time.

Then comes the job of drying with a large towel. Get the Afghan 'towel-dry' as much as possible before using the hair dryer. And a word here about dryers. You can use the ordinary domestic kind, but they really will not stand up to the sustained length of drying time most Afghans need, and I would suggest investing in an industrial type of hair dryer, either hand model or preferably one on a stand which then leaves both hands free for grooming.

Choose a hair dryer with a gusty blow. Work a small area at a time, starting with the head and ears, and then the neck, body and legs. Thoroughly dry each area before moving on. This a slow process and needs patience, but the reward is tremendous. You must allow two or three hours for bathing and grooming and drying an adult Afghan.

The dog should be dried in warm surroundings. It is going to take time and it is very easy for the Afghan to catch a chill when wet. Direct the blower-dryer to an area of the coat which will be lifted and then you will be able to groom with your brush right through to the roots. Smooth down the coat before moving on to the next area.

This is our way of bathing an Afghan – and it is the same for a pet or show dog, except, of course, that it is essential for the show Afghan to be kept in a clean state. If you bath your Afghan for a show do it not more than 24 hours before the show, and do be careful to keep it clean. I am amazed at owners who have spent hours bathing and grooming their dogs only to let them lie about on a filthy dog show floor. Why bother to bath unless you are going to benefit by taking a clean Afghan into the ring? Remember that you have not finished the job until your dog is completely and thoroughly dry, and so far you have only used your wire-pin brush. The grooming can now be finished off by combing, and this will take out any tiny tangles or knots in the coat. This is important because within a few days these can develop into large mats.

As part of the bathing process we swab out the ears with cotton wool to remove any moisture and to keep them clean. And you can also check the teeth and remove any tartar. You can buy a scraping tool for this that is easy to use. Never use hair lacquer on the Afghan's coat. This makes it much too brittle and it will easily break off, resulting in a noticeable loss.

Well, at the end of all this you should have a really good looking Afghan that you can proudly exhibit to your family and friends, and in the show ring you will surely catch the judge's eye and maybe win a prize card. A lot of hard work and time goes into the preparation of an Afghan — but at the end a beautiful looking Afghan that is a joy to own makes it all worthwhile.

Red dog

Exhibiting and show training

Every registered Afghan is eligible to be exhibited at a dog show. There is no colour bar, and as long as your dog moves on all four legs you have a chance of winning a prize. There is really no such thing as a 'pet' or 'show' Afghan. The terms are used but it is all a matter of opinion.

I well remember attending my first Championship show and winning quite well with my two bitches. On the way home we stopped for a meal and met some Afghan folk travelling North. One of them was a judge. 'I liked your black and tan', he said, 'but that golden one is strictly a pet. You should save your money and leave it at home'. The golden one had won the first prize and had beaten one of his dogs. She later became Champion Zaza of Khorrassan and Afghan of the Year. So much for his assessment of a pet Afghan!

Show appearances the world over have increased enormously in the last ten years and at most shows Afghans now have the leading number of entries. The show bug is infectious and bites hard with a lasting effect. I claim that irrespective of your Afghan's qualities, you have only to show often enough to become a prize winner. Sadly the quality of judging is poor in my experience and the variation in awards is wide and generous. To me this is proof of poor judging. But it certainly makes life interesting for the 'pet' Afghan!

I have been fortunate in my own kennel to have some very good natural show dogs. I never intensely trained them for the show ring and they were happy enough to show naturally and win prizes. But a certain amount of training will help you in the ring.

Get your Afghan used to being handled by as many people as possible. Encourage people to stroke the dog, and a tickle under the chin helps to keep that proud head held high.

A puppy can be shown at most shows at six months of age. For a month or so before get the puppy used to being placed properly on the ground. It should stand on all four legs in a natural pose. Make sure that the front legs are not too close together giving the impression they both come out of one hole; neither should they be too far apart giving a pyramid front.

It is a common fault to see the front legs pulled too far forward which sometimes creates a sagging topline. The front egs should be slightly under, but to the fore of the shoulders. The back legs should not be too far back as this again can dip he topline and be uncomfortable for the dog. The back feet should be placed to show a good but not exaggerated angulation, not too far apart but a little more than the width of the body. This stance is perfectly natural for the adult Afghan, but the young dog may need some persuasion to stand correctly. Watch that neither front nor back feet are turned with toes in or out. They should be straight ahead.

The tail is allowed to be up or down when standing. In America some handlers hold the tail raised. This is generally frowned upon in England but I personally think it makes an attractive picture. If the tail is tucked firmly between the legs, this is a sign that the dog is unhappy. A word whispered in the ear might help or scratching gently between the hip bones sometimes gets the tail in a happier position.

Watch the topline. If it sags (a fault) it could be the result of standing incorrectly or perhaps of standing on uneven ground. But do not be too fussy with your dog. If your Afghan is standing correctly *leave it alone.*

I do not like to see the head strung up by a lead, as seen in the terrier ring. If the Afghan is happy it will not be necessary to pull the head up. If you do you will almost certainly see the tail tucked at the other end.

When your Afghan is standing happily smooth down the coat with a brush – but do it quickly. Judges do not usually like to see exhibitors constantly grooming their dog in the show ring. Do not let your dog lie down in the ring.

With a young puppy the important thing is to keep it happy. Winning a prize card on the first outing is very exciting, but not essential. At the risk of annoying the judge, play with your puppy in the ring. *Relax!* If you are tense you will transmit this to the dog and he won't show off properly at all. Try to attend a dog show to see how other handlers and judges behave. Most judges want the dog to stand still and allow them to examine teeth (to look for the level or scissor bite), feel over the head, across the skull, the ear set. Then to run their hands down the neck. All this is done in front of the dog so make sure your Afghan gets used to people handling him from the front and in close proximity. The judge will then move to the side of the dog to feel the shoulder placement, exerting slight pressure to test that the elbows do not splay outward, running his hand down the front leg to feel the bone and the front foot to assess the size, and then along the back, perhaps exerting a little pressure on the back to test for any slackness. The judge then moves to the rear feeling hip bones and the angulation of the rear legs. And finally he will want to feel the placement of the tail and the end ring, and the judge may raise the tail.

Again, get your dog used to someone standing behind it.

The judge may then move to the side of the dog and back several paces to assess the standing position. Your dog should stand still taking no interest in him at all. You should keep one eye on the judge and one on the dog. If your Afghan starts shuffling its feet around — *DON'T PANIC.* Gently put the feet back in position, whispering calmly to the dog. Remember! The judge's eye is on you as well as on the dog. If you start trembling now the dog will feel this and will worry. Take it easy and be calm. If your Afghan suddenly falls to pieces, sits down, scratches itself, or even evacuates its bladder and bowels, you may have lost your chance of a prize this time, but the dog is still yours. It is not condemned for ever.

After the judge has inspected your dog you will then be asked to move it. Afghans should be judged in movement from the rear, side and front. When I judge I ask exhibitors to move their dogs in a large triangle which gives me a proper opportunity to assess movement. The stylish movement of the Afghan is important to catch the judge's eye, but when you practise, use different surfaces such as grass, gravel, soil, carpet, lino, floorboards and tarmac. The surfaces of show rings vary so it is as well to be prepared. Move fairly briskly, but do not run. Walk in front of your dog with a slack lead under the chin. A little tug of the lead will encourage the head to be raised.

When you move in the ring keep an eye on where you are going so that you don't bump into a fellow exhibitor or another dog, and always keep an eye on your dog. So many handlers forge ahead, never looking at their dog, and never knowing that its head was down or it was moving like a crab. If you are watching your dog carefully you can correct any faulty movement that develops and give a little encouragement if the tail is slow in coming up on the move — an important show point.

Allow yourself plenty of room when standing your dog with others in the ring. Do not go too near the dog in front and keep

This represents British show stance; in the USA the stance differs by the tail being held up as shown by the broken line

Table

"New" dogs (unseen by Judge)

Handler

Dog being examined by Judge

Judge

"Old" dogs (already seen by Judge in a previous class)

Table

Judge

All dogs

"Once round, please"

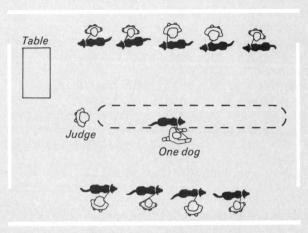

"Once up and down, please"

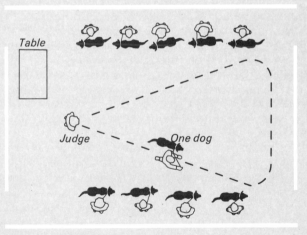

"Triangle, please"

65

away from the dog behind. And never give up presenting your dog to the judge. if you are pulled out among the winners the job is not yet finished. Make sure your dog is standing correctly at all times in the ring and be certain there isn't a hair out of place. And do all this without unnecessary fuss. If you are standing first in line don't take it for granted that you are the judge's selection for a first prize. Judges can change their minds at the last moment.

Wear sensible shoes for high heels have no place in the dog show ring, and wear clothing that doesn't flap around and distract and upset your dog. In the end, of course, close adherence to the breed standard wins the top prizes but the behaviour of you and your dog is the thing that first catches the judge's attention.

If you think about it the whole judging process, of someone feeling over the bones and shape of an Afghan, is really very foreign and distasteful to the dog. It may be necessary but it's hardly dignified to be handled all over by a stranger. And yet that is what we expect our Afghans to suffer and pretend not to be bothered.

A final word about dog shows. There are winners, but there are a greater number of losers. Be careful how you behave in the ring if you win or lose. To gloat over someone when you win is as unsporting as to be furious with an exhibitor when you lose. Never speak to the judge unless he asks a question of you. The show ring is charged with emotion. After all, this is the culmination of months of training and hours of hard work in grooming and presenting your Afghan to perfection. If you lose, your first thought might be – 'What a waste of time'. But there is always another show to attend and another judge to try out.

Don't mark down a judge who doesn't place your dog as someone never to risk again. A judge can change his mind, and if he is a fair person he will judge a dog on that day only. And every dog has its off day.

I am often asked, 'What do you think of my dog?' What exhibitors usually mean is, 'Would you give my dog a first prize if you were judge?' The question is unanswerable. A dog has to be judged on the day and by comparison with other dogs in the class. Unfortunately too many judges the world over judge on 'type'. They are in favour of a certain type of dog, irrespective of virtues or faults, and a dog varying from their wn type preference is not fairly considered. This is a very bad method of judging but it does happen, and many newcomers are put off exhibiting their dogs because of these judges.

When can you finally assess whether you have a 'show' Afghan or whether your Affie is really a 'pet' and not designed for the show ring? Well, I think you would have to show under at least a dozen different judges at a dozen different shows, and even then you might not be certain.

Some puppies win a great number of prizes during their puppyhood (six to twelve months), but never mature into good adult specimens. Other puppies win very little when young and yet become Champions.

Many an ugly duckling makes a very fine swan.

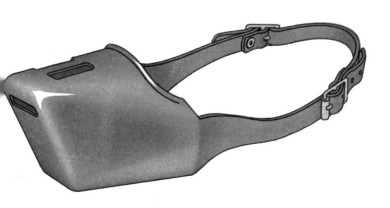

Muzzle of moulded plastic which can be sterilized and used as an anti-rabies measure

Breeding

Selecting a suitable dog to breed to your bitch is not an easy job. Too many breeders are anxious to press upon you the services of their own stud dogs and you can get much differing advice as to which stud dog would be best for your bitch. My advice would be to go back to your bitch's breeder for help. A pedigree does count for a lot but so does the physical make-up of a dog. You really want a mixture of a well bred dog that is also a good looking specimen. It is not easy to find such a dog.

Somewhere along the line you will probably ask yourself, 'Should I breed for colour?' The answer ought to be, 'No!' For a pet the main thing is temperament which we have already discussed. In a show specimen you are trying to breed close to the standard of points and – as it clearly says in all standards – any colour is acceptable.

One could write a book about Afghan colour, and indeed there are many interesting volumes on colour breeding in dogs. But in the Afghan, colour is a bonus and not an essential requirement.

The colour spectrum in the breed is almost limitless – Reds, Goldens, Fawns, Creams, Whites, Ivories, Silvers, Blacks, Black and Tans, Black and Silvers, Blues, Brindles. The Kennel Club will accept any colour for registration and, as proof of this, we once sold a Cream Afghan to a young couple who had always wanted a 'Champagne Afghan'. So we registered the dog as 'Champagne' in colour, and this was accepted by the Kennel Club!

Up to the early 1960s Black and Black and Tan were not in vogue and many breeders culled this colour at birth. There were Black and Tan Champions before this time, but a Black colour or combination *was* difficult to sell. The scene changed when my home bred Champion Tara of Pooghan came into the show ring. She was a very good Afghan, a natural for shows and a lovable clown, who won seventeen best puppy awards in top competition. When breeders and exhibitors realised you could win with a dog of her colour it created renewed interest, and for a while the Black and Tan/Silver came into fashion and has remained popular in the show ring.

The brindle became popular by way of American imports into many European countries, despite the fact that this colour vexed some breeders for a while and many thought it detracted from the Oriental expression. But many brindles won very well throughout the late 1960s and early 70s, although there is some indication at the time of writing that the popularity has waned.

There are Champions in all the colours I have mentioned and obviously judges are now prepared to accept any colour. This was not always so. Indeed I was once told by the owner of a famous Black and Tan Champion that one judge in Scotland put her dog last in the class, telling her the colour was improper.

In breeding, black is a very dominant colour. But the colours are so mixed behind almost every dog's pedigree that it is safe to say that any colour is likely in turn to breed any colour. For instance there are Black and Tan dogs who are credited with siring nothing but Golden puppies. But if you use a black dog at stud you will probably find his colour is dominant. The golden dog does not appear to be as dominant and will usually produce a variety of colours and colour combinations. The white dog is quite dominant, and if there are a good number of puppies in a litter with white breeding behind it you will nearly always find a white puppy. Not of course an albino. I have never heard of an albino Afghan.

Colour breeding in practical terms does not exist in Afghans. If you talk to genetic researchers they will admit that you would have to breed the same dog to the same bitch 1,000 times to prove colour genetic theory completely!

While I am writing about colour I must make mention of the black face or mask, which is so often wrongly preferred by judges. I say wrongly because it is improper to regard this as a breed point. The argument often persists that a black mask makes a true expression, but you very often fail to find this in Salukis and many plain faced dogs have the desired Eastern expression.

Do not bother about colour when selecting a stud dog for your bitch, and do not, for goodness' sake, decide on the Afghan in the next street simply because it is the most convenient dog available. There is no point in breeding a litter of Afghan puppies just for the sake of it. It is much more important, and interesting too, to breed a good litter of pups that will be a credit to you as the breeder.

You should start looking for the stud dog for your bitch some time before she is ready for mating. Be prepared, if necessary, to travel to the other end of the country if you genuinely believe the most suitable dog lives there. Examine the dog's pedigree. A string of Champions in his ancestral line does not necessarily make him a great stud dog. What is of more interest is a definite 'line' of breeding. This might show itself in his sire and dam, or more likely his grandsire and grandam, having parents registered with the same kennel prefix. This usually indicates that an effort has been made to line-breed the dog.

Examine your bitch's pedigree also, and you may well match up a similar breeding pattern back to the third, fourth or fifth generation. Then you will have to discover if this matching pedigree contains good dogs and bitches because, if you double up on the breeding, the dominance of the same ancestors will come through to your litter of puppies.

If your bitch's pedigree contains the same Afghans as the proposed stud dog, and if those animals had undesirable characteristics, they will show in your puppies; but the opposite is also the case. If they were really outstanding specimens you should get puppies with some of their virtues.

It is fair to say that if you do not like the look of the stud dog you will be disappointed in the puppies he produces, and one of the best methods of assessing a stud dog's potential is to look at his progeny in the show ring. There are many things to take into consideration when selecting a stud dog but if you use a Champion merely because of his title, you are almost certainly on the wrong lines.

I remember someone once coming up to me moaning bitterly that a fairly well known Champion dog had sired puppies just like himself – and the person complaining detested that type of dog! Well, why use the dog? An additional problem is that nature doesn't always balance out faults and virtues. If your bitch has a thick head and you mate her to a fine headed dog you may be lucky to get the balance you are seeking but you are more liable to get half your puppies with thick heads and the other half with fine. On the other hand it is safe to predict that if your bitch has a prominent fault and the selected stud dog has the same fault – the puppies will have that fault to a degree.

Let me tell you what we do in our own kennel when there is a stud inquiry. We ask to look at the bitch's pedigree and compare it with the pedigrees of our own team of stud dogs. I

70

have a good idea of which ancestors to avoid when doubling up on breeding, and I would point this out to a bitch's owner. I would hope to show some of my stud dog's progeny and nearly always, in the end, it comes down to the use of one of two dogs. The final choice is always left to the owner of the bitch but I would never let any stud dog of mine be used where I thought the breeding was unsuitable because of mismatching pedigrees or faults.

Having chosen a stud dog you should prepare the bitch for breeding. A bitch should never be mated before fifteen months of age, although she usually has her first season between six months and a year. This varies considerably and I have known Afghans to have a first season at the age of two years. This does not mean that the bitch is deformed (I once heard an 'expert' tell a novice this). It could be that the bitch has had a season earlier that was not detected.

Allow your bitch to come into season naturally. I am very much against injections to bring a season on because these 'seasons' are sometimes false and there are no resulting puppies. To my mind there is always the danger of affecting internal organs, sometimes with fatal results. The whole breeding process is a natural one and has gone on for thousands of years so try to keep it that way!

Overweight is sometimes a problem and results in loss of fertility. But if you are at all uncertain about the health of your bitch take veterinary advice and have a check up. Your vet would be able to tell you, for instance, about any vitamin deficiency.

The start of the season should be shown by an enlarged vulva and, after a few days, there will be a bloody discharge. Most bitches are very clean and take care of themselves and in my experience I have found that they do not seem to attract local dogs to their door as strongly as other breeds. But, of course, great care should be taken that on no account does your bitch mix with any other dog, other than the chosen stud dog, for the full 21 days of her season cycle. We suggest worming a bitch at the start of her season, which should not upset things in any way, providing the worming medicine is obtained from the vet. Worms in puppies are a great problem and account for a high mortality rate. Worming your bitch prior to mating should reduce the incidence of worms.

Do not bath the bitch before mating. The smells surrounding

her may be offensive to you but they will attract the stud dog. But a grooming before the mating will not come amiss. A well groomed Afghan bitch is more likely to please the owner of the stud dog than a bitch that is matted solid.

If you have previously selected a stud dog, advise the owner that your bitch has come into season on her first day, that is the first day of the actual discharge. Your bitch will be ready on her tenth day and, if possible, you should try a second mating, particularly for a maiden bitch, on the twelfth day. By the time your bitch is ready for mating the bloody discharge may have cleared up but there will probably be a clear discharge, hardly noticeable, and the vulva will still be swollen. A very basic test is to stand your bitch and scratch between the hip bones. If she is ready for mating she will usually twitch her tail to the side. This is a fairly crude but effective way of seeing if she is ready for her mate.

You should travel your bitch to the dog because she is less likely to be affected by strange surroundings than the stud dog.

If a stud dog is experienced, the mating should not be difficult. We usually ask the owner of a bitch to go into another room because their presence is likely to upset her, but we always ask the owner to see the bitch 'tied' to the dog as proof that mating has taken place. This tying process can take from 5 minutes to (on odd and highly inconvenient occasions!) as much as an hour. The length of tie has nothing to do with the effectiveness of mating and sometimes an outside tie occurs. This is not desirable but I have known many litters of puppies conceived in this way.

I must say a word here about the payment of the stud fee. Ask about this at the first inquiry about the use of the stud dog. Most breeders have a set fee for their dogs or an arrangement can be made to take a puppy from the litter instead of a fee.

Paying a fee is a better and neater method, but if an arrangement is made about taking a puppy the owner of the dog will usually want the 'pick of litter', that is the best puppy in the litter chosen by the stud dog owner. This can be selected at any time up to eight weeks of age, or at an age specified by the owner of the dog. It would be improper of you to sell any puppy until the pick of litter is chosen and, remember, this can be highly inconvenient to you. The onus is on *you* to take the puppies to the stud dog owner to select his puppy. Again, this can be highly inconvenient if you have to transport perhaps half a dozen eight-week-old puppies some distance! A pick of litter puppy is usually unregistered, which means that although you will be listed as the breeder, it may carry the stud dog owner's kennel prefix with its name.

You can see how complicated it is to make an arrangement about giving a puppy instead of paying a fee, and it is well to understand the drawbacks of this method of obtaining the stud dog's services. On the other hand, if you pay a fee, remember the fee is solely for the use of the stud dog. There is no guarantee of puppies resulting from the mating and you do not have the right to demand your money back or insist on a mating during the next season. Usually, at the time of mating, the owner of the dog will offer a free mating next time if no puppies are forthcoming, but this is a concession, not a right. If there are no puppies it would be impossible to apportion the blame. It could be an off day for the dog, but you could not prove this. It could be the wrong day for the bitch but you will never know. There is a very high fertility rate with Afghans and the chances are that a good mating will produce a litter of puppies. But this is not necessarily automatic!

The care of the bitch during pregnancy is very important. The quantity of food should be increased, and, perhaps more important, its quality should be improved if you want healthy babies. The gestation period is sixty-one to sixty-three days, give or take two days either side. You should mark off the sixty-one and sixty-three days from the first mating. In our kennel we give a gradual increase in food from two weeks after mating. Each morning the bitch will have a raw egg mixed with milk and we feed the prescribed quantity of Canovel tablets obtained from the vet.

The pregnancy will go slowly if this is your first litter. The first real sign that there are puppies will be a slight fattening of the belly and a slight swelling of the nipples. Towards the end of her pregnancy the bitch will probably lie on her side with her belly fully distended and you can see the puppies quite clearly moving in her womb.

Before the end of the pregnancy her bed should be prepared. We recommend buying an electrically heated fibre glass bed — 40in. (100cm.) x 24in. (60cm.). This is a sound investment and the additional bonus of constant heat for the babies might well save the lives of some of them. If the puppies are going to be

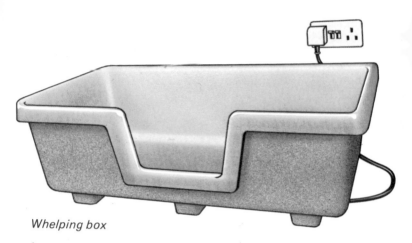

Whelping box

born in warm weather and it is felt that additional heat is unnecessary make up a sturdy wooden box. Get the bitch used to going to the box towards the end of her pregnancy and she will soon realise this is her nest.

About two weeks before the puppies are due, take your bitch to a poodle parlour and ask them to shave the hair around her teats. This must be done *gently,* but it is a professional job with electric clippers. There is no need to cut or shave any more coat than this.

When the puppies are due you will find the bitch getting restless and perhaps panting a little. The final sign is that she will refuse food and empty herself. If it is her first litter she might start to whine. This is not necessarily due to pain. I think it is a mixture of trying to get attention from you and some uncertainty about what is happening to her. The final stage is the bearing down trying to expel the first puppy. The contractions will be quite strong from the beginning and the vulva will open slightly. It is quite normal for contractions to last up to half an hour. If they go on for more than an hour without a puppy being born it would be wise to call your vet. In any case most vets will not mind being warned a day or so in advance that there are puppies due. The first puppy is sometimes passed with a little difficulty. If you want to help, watch the contractions. If these go on for some time and a puppy is emerging and then disappearing again, on its next emergence gently hold the puppy and gently, *very gently,* pull as the push comes from the bitch.

The puppy is born in a bag of fluid and the bitch will usually tear this apart. Attached to the bag is the placenta or afterbirth and the bitch will want to eat this. Frankly it is best to let her as it is believed to contain susstances that stimulate her milk supply. It is fairly disgusting to watch the bitch eating afterbirth, but if you take it away from her she may get distressed searching for it. Check that after each puppy is born an afterbirth comes away from the bitch. Your vet may ask you about this afterwards. The bitch will bite off the umbilical cord and although the puppy may bleed a little she will usually clear this up. The bitch herself should not bleed too much at the birth of a puppy but a certain amount of fluid containing blood may be discharged with a sudden gush. Do not be concerned about this. And don't be worried if it is green in colour as this is fairly common. After the first puppy the remainder should follow fairly easily at twenty to thirty minute intervals. But this can vary and you can have a puppy every five minutes or at intervals of an hour or two hours. The bitch will not need a great deal of help for she has a natural instinct to care for her puppies, licking each one into life. The puppy makes straight away for a teat, and within minutes it will be feeding from its mother before the next puppy is born.

Afghans can have large litters and it is impossible to quote an average number. I have known bitches have a single puppy, but it is common for them to produce as many as fifteen.

It is terribly difficult for me to tell you about culling puppies, if it is felt that there are too many for the bitch to manage comfortably. If they are all healthy how can you start to sort them out? You may be destroying a future Champion, or you may be getting rid of the poor doer that will be a constant problem to feed and rear. I know that not all breeders agree with me, but I am in favour of letting nature take its course. However many puppies are born, put them to the bitch. She will push aside the unhealthy and weak. This does not mean that you should not give some assistance. If you see a puppy that is not getting its fair share of the rations push it on to a teat. But I am not in favour of slaving over a brood of puppies day and night. It is upsetting when the weaker puppies die but perhaps nature intended it that way.

I may be painting an unduly gloomy picture here, because the truth is that the Afghan is a good mother, her puppies are usually healthy, and very few fail to survive.

But the problem of weakly puppies is a somewhat controversial one. Should you work on a puppy twenty-four hours a day feeding it all the time every two hours? It is up to you. Don't get the impression that we leave the puppies alone with a 'survival of the fittest' attitude. The puppies have to be carefully watched all the time. If your bitch has a heavy coat the puppies can easily tangle themselves up in this and strangle themselves. We check a bitch every half hour during the day and evening, but if all is well we leave her alone through the night.

When the bitch appears to have had her final puppy, call in your veterinary surgeon to check her over and perhaps give her an injection of pituitan which will usually start her gently contracting to expel another puppy, if there is one, or any afterbirth left inside. This is important because, if anything is left inside, it will rot very quickly and cause a lot of problems. The vet may also give the bitch an antibiotic injection as a precaution.

If the bitch has eaten her afterbirth her motions will be very black and very smelly for a few days, but she will soon be back to normal. It is important to give her plenty of water. Opinions seem to vary about giving her milk. We give our bitches a lot of milk when they first have puppies but some breeders say this can scour the bitch and cause digestive upsets. Certainly clean, fresh water is a definite requirement. And the bitch's diet while nursing her litter should be of high protein and good quality. Scraps of food are not to be given during this period.

Inform the owner of the stud dog when all the puppies are born giving details of number, colours (if they are obvious at this age) and sexes. Don't be too bothered about the colours of the newly born pups for they can be very deceptive. Silvers are sometimes born black; black and tans are usually that colour at birth but reds and goldens can sometimes be black or a muddy brown colour. Very often colours are not positive until about four weeks of age. You examine the roots of what very little coat there is on a puppy and it is the colour of the roots that will give a clue as to the final colour of the youngster. But I must warn you that one of our first litters of pups contained what we thought was a very attractive black and tan and it stayed that way for weeks before turning into an equally attractive deep golden colour.

The bitch will be very protective and will not usually tolerate strangers anywhere near her babies. The immediate family, the people she knows well, are acceptable, but it is not a good idea at this stage to bring in friends and neighbours to look at the new arrivals. Respect your bitch's natural desire to protect her pups and be grateful for it because it is a sign that she will be a good mother. She will not want to leave them at all in the beginning and may have to be persuaded to leave the whelping box to attend to calls of nature.

Right from birth cleanliness is essential for survival of puppies. We find the best bedding for the baby Afghans is newspaper shredded into tiny pieces. It is warm, absorbent, and easy to clear up. A mild disinfectant should be used to wash the whelping box at least twice a day.

Do not be disturbed if you see the bitch eating the puppy's motions. This may be disagreeable to you, but is perfectly natural to her. You will also see the bitch licking the puppy's undersides a great deal. This is a two-fold action; she is establishing ownership of the pup and assisting its digestive system.

The breed standard allows the dew claws to be taken off or left on. These are the small claws slightly up from the rear and front paws. You must never take these off yourself. Call in your vet to do it if you feel it is necessary to be done. We leave the dew claws alone as they rarely cause trouble in the adult Afghan.

After a week or so, the bitch may start leaving the puppies for a short while. This is where the heated fibre glass bed is so useful because puppies must be kept warm at all times. The bitch should be gently encouraged back to her puppies because, if she is allowed to leave them for long periods, she may lose interest in them.

When all the puppies are born they should be examined carefully, one by one. Abnormalities are very rare in Afghan puppies but if it is felt necessary to destroy a puppy this *must* be done by a vet. The abnormalities that can occur are incorrectly formed head, body or legs. Look out for cleft palates. The symptoms are noisy breathing and a tendency to blow bubbles. But these abnormalities are *rare* and they probably will not occur in any of your puppies. But if they do, get veterinary advice. There is no point in letting a puppy affected by an abnormality suffer all its life.

At two and a half to three weeks of age it is time to start

weaning the puppies. Their first meal will be a milky feed such as warm milk mixed with a little glucose and baby cereal. But it must not be made too thick at first. Place the puppies round the dishes and *gently* dip in their noses. Be careful here because it would be easy to get food into their lungs. They will usually lick their noses and, if they like the taste, they will look for the source of the food. The mother should be kept away from puppy food because she has no respect for the puppy's needs at this time and will eat it herself. Incidentally if you see the mother vomiting food near her puppies don't be too disturbed. This is a natural action and she is merely offering them pre-digested food. But this should not be encouraged and when the puppies are weaning you should not put the mother straight to her puppies immediately after feeding her. Allow her time to digest her food completely.

The eyes open at ten days but it is a day or two before the puppies can actually see fully. With luck you should have no weaning problems and when you start to feed the puppies yourself you have an opportunity to start balancing them up. A puppy that may be a little on the thin side should now get more attention from you to get it up to its brothers and sisters in strength and size.

Care and patience is needed when introducing puppies to food but as soon as possible get the puppies on to five meals a day as described in the section General Care, Feeding. By the age of six weeks they should be able to do without their mother's milk, but if Mum still wants to feed them and take care of them there is no harm in this. Remember at eight weeks they should be ready for their new homes and must be independent of their mother well before this.

When the puppies are about four weeks of age, and the colour is showing properly and all is well, I suggest you start to advertise them in your local newspaper and in the dog papers.

AFGHAN PUPPIES FOR SALE
Dam: . . . .
Sire: . . . .
Reds, Goldens, Silvers and Black and Tans.
Dogs and bitches available. Well reared.
Price: . . . .
Apply: (your name, address and 'phone number).

Do not make extravagant claims or promises in advertising. A simply worded advertisment that makes sense to anyone interested in buying an Afghan might be as shown.

All the relevant information is there. It would be stupid of you to describe them as 'show' puppies. They just do not exist! Listing the show winnings of sire and dam is really superfluous, unless the winning was at top level and consistent. Do have a price for your puppies and remember it is quite costly to wean and rear puppies properly, so the asking price should be fair. You also have to consider the cost of the stud fee and any veterinary attention. Under no circumstances sell your puppies to a dealer for re-sale.

While the bitch is with her puppies it is difficult to keep her groomed. We let our bitches mat up and try to rescue as much coat as possible when the pups are about three to four weeks old. If the bitch gets very messed up while actually having the puppies it might be wise to bathe her back end after a couple of days, but return her to her puppies quickly. And make sure she is fully dry before returning to her puppies.

When you get inquiries about the puppies invite prospective owners to come and see them at three to four weeks of age. Make sure the person wanting the puppy has the time to care for it properly and there is adequate housing. You must point out the drawbacks of the Afghan, as well as the virtues. You will regret it if you 'over sell' a puppy. It is best to be businesslike when selling puppies. Take a deposit from the prospective owner which will secure the puppy for him. The full balance must be paid when the puppy is collected at eight weeks of age. On no account arrange 'terms'. If someone can't afford a puppy, the chances are that they are unable to feed it and care for it properly. Make proper arrangements regarding the money side of the transaction and there can be no complaints afterwards of any bad dealing.

Before you advertise the puppies for sale, you must make up your mind whether you intend keeping a puppy from the litter for yourself. You already have a bitch and you must think carefully before keeping a male because of the problems when the bitch comes in season. Afghans reveal incestuous tendencies from an early age!

A word about the relationship between the bitch and her puppies is appropriate here. Let them play together because this is an important part of the puppy's upbringing and its development. Get the pups used to being handled by humans from about five to six weeks of age. Children can be very helpful here, though you must be on the look out for any maltreatment by youngsters. This human contact is most important and has great influence on subsequent temperament.

Always allow the prospective buyer to select freely from the puppies that are available, but those already spoken for must be pointed out. Do not persuade a buyer to take a colour other than the one he wants. You must sell a puppy honestly otherwise the consequences can be painful. Try tactfully to discover why the prospective buyer wants a puppy. Is it the novelty value? If so, don't sell. One of the problems of the breed is that so many are sold to improper homes, and the result is an unwanted Afghan that goes from home to home or ends up in an animal welfare shelter, destined for destruction.

Be careful how you sell a puppy and to whom you sell a puppy. If you can tell on the telephone that someone is unsuitable as an owner put them off by saying you will write to them. If someone visits your home and again you feel they are unsuitable suggest that perhaps an Afghan is not the sort of dog they need and suggest another breed. I once had a great problem with a gentleman who threatened to sue me if I did not sell him a puppy! I did not sell him one – and he did not take me to the law courts!

In this chapter on breeding I have dealt almost exclusively with bitches and puppies. What advice can I give the owner of a male dog about using it at stud? First you should consider whether your dog is really a good enough specimen to breed from. I think most bitches are adequate and faults can be rectified by the use of suitable dogs. But a dog of insignificant breeding and of not much virtue in terms of breed points should not, in my view, be used at stud even though he may be a splendid pet. There should be a purpose in breeding, and while I feel that a litter may be good for the well being of an Afghan bitch I cannot say the same about the male dog. A bitch never used for breeding may have problems in later life but this is not so with a dog. And a dog that is used at stud can be a nuisance in the home, particularly if there are any bitches in the neighbourhood.

I am not advocating that stud work should be left exclusively to the bigger kennels, but I would recommend that a pet dog is

ot used at stud unless it has some outstanding qualities. Do
not breed puppies just for the sake of it. The purpose should be
to improve the breed and to improve your own stock. But if you
are using your dog at stud make sure it is healthy, neither too
fat nor too thin. Keep it in good condition and pay particular
attention to its coat. No one is interested in an untidy, uncared
for dog. Breeding is a serious business but if offers immense
satisfaction. There is a particular thrill in achieving your first
litter of Afghan puppies, watching them grow and perhaps in
later life seeing them in the show ring.

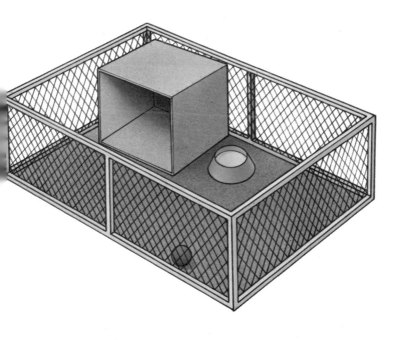

Puppy pen

The breed worldwide

I am fortunate in owning the top winning Afghan of all time in England. International Champion Tzara of Pooghan has attracted visitors to my kennel from all over the world and this has given me an insight into the breed world wide and I know personally that the Afghan Hound is a resident in over 40 countries in the world, and the popularity of the breed extends from China to Columbia and from Greece to Greenland.

Until the end of the nineteenth century Afghans were found only in Afghanistan and Northern India – they came to Britain where they made no headway as a distinct breed until the early 1920s. In the late 20s the Afghan was imported from its native country into neighbouring territories and at about the same time English bred dogs were starting to travel the world. In 1928 Hans Jungeling introduced them into Holland and around the same time the Marx Brothers brought them into America. In the U.S.A. the breed tended to be bought for its novelty value in the first instance among the Hollywood community.

The initial interest in Afghans seemed to dwindle after a very short time, but in the late 1930s a number of exports from England again travelled the world and most countries seem to trace their Afghan history from this time. The best way to research the breed's history in different countries is to discover when it was given Championship status because this will tell you when sufficient numbers were registered to qualify for recognition. Most countries 'recognised' Afghans by 1940 but Britain led the way by giving them their status as early as 1926.

The countries strongest in Afghans at the time of writing are Britain and America. Both nations get more than 200 Afghans to a show. Closely following are Australia, Finland, Sweden, Holland, Belgium and France where 50 to 100 Afghans are seen at a single show. Britain has, however, topped the 400 mark, and this has occurred in America as well.

Most countries acknowledge that England sent out their basic stock. It must be admitted however that until fairly recent times it was inferior stock that *sometimes* reached them. I do not wish to condemn unfairly here, but when I started in Afghans in 1960 I had an early inquiry for a puppy to go to Australia and a top breeder at the time said, "Don't send the best in your litter under any circumstances". I found this to be a general view, but of course some very good dogs were also sent out to various countries earlier on.

Most of the world's nations classify Afghans at their shows but the number of shows in a given country varies considerably. As I write, England has about 35 Championship shows with Afghan classes. There are 300 in Australia. Different quarantine regulations world-wide restrict appearances. There are very strict quarantine laws in Britain, for example, and that means that no dogs from this country can travel outside the British Isles to attend shows. Incoming dogs spend 6 months or so in quarantine kennels which virtually prohibits International dog showing in Britain.

In the rest of Europe it is a little different. Dogs can travel freely between Denmark, Holland, Belgium, Germany, Luxembourg, France, Spain, Italy and Portugal. The only restriction is a financial one because it is expensive to travel in different countries, but the top European dogs do manage to 'make the rounds' and one dog I exported won 17 Certificates in half a dozen countries with some ease.

The Scandinavian countries of Finland, Sweden and Norway have quarantine restrictions which make it impractical for European dogs to travel and exhibit at shows within their boundaries. A few years ago, when restrictions were not so stringent, the Scaninavian dogs were making forays into Europe and doing some useful winning.

Throughout the world there are two different ways that a dog becomes a Champion, either by winning a certain number of certificates or on a points basis. In most European countries a dog has to win three certificates at three separate shows under three different judges to become a Champion of that country. In Ireland the award is the Green Star, which is worth so many points depending on the number of dogs at a show. In America a points system is in operation, as it is in Australia, but in both countries top wins at four shows can give you a Champion's title.

From the 1920s to the 1960s Britain led the way with exports, but from the late 1960s to the present time America has been exporting hounds to Australia, Europe and Scandinavia, and now there are few countries in the world where Afghans do not carry a mixture of English and American blood.

I have judged in the three Scandianavian countries and was

interested to see how well the American imported hounds had blended with the existing stock. Many virtues were to be seen when Scandinavian breeders bred carefully chosen stock to the American imports. I found when judging in Holland and Belgium that there was much less American influence. The breed was dominated from the 1940s to the early 1970s by Miss Eta Pauptit's Oranje Manege kennels. Miss Pauptit enthused about the Ghazni type of dogs, and was far more interested in breeding Afghans that could do their original job of hunting and racing, than glamorously coated hounds with poor shapes underneath. When I spoke to her she was critical of British Afghans and even more critical of the Americans. Certainly her Afghans were very typical breed specimens and were difficult to fault.

In recent years England has been the Mecca for Afghan owners and the high quality presentation that became the vogue in England in the 1960s was taken up round the world. The exception was America where the Afghan exhibitors have been conscious of the value of presentation for many years. I think it is fair to say that prior to 1970 high quality presentation and grooming was only to be seen in England and America, but the change has been fast and dramatic. In a five year period of judging in Sweden and other Continental countries I saw great differences, and in many countries I saw grooming and presentation that left a great deal to be desired change almost overnight into a competent job.

England may have ruled the roost for several decades with Afghan breeding and showing, but a disturbing feature of my many travels abroad was the discovery that a number of English judges were downing any stock in the country in which they were judging if it did not come from their own kennel. A great deal of harm has been done by many breed judges who acted as though any stock in a country other than England was inferior. I was happy to report to my Continental friends in many instances that many of these judges had little standing in their homeland.

When judging abroad I did find that many Continental judges had a number of fads that made their judging suspect. In several countries a dog must have a full set of teeth. This has never been necessary in England and America and is not mentioned in the breed standard, but I have seen a number of good dogs passed over by German and Belgian judges because pre-molars were missing. It is a point to remember if you ever get a puppy inquiry from countries that insist on a full denture.

In many countries Afghans are raced as much as they are shown in the ring, and racing is now becoming part of the Afghan scene. Early Afghan racing started in the 1930s and by all accounts there were some amusing times. At one race track in England when Afghans were first run, the hare was caught because the Afghans worked out that there was little point in chasing it round the circular track when you could cut across the middle ground and head it off. And this they did, to the amusement of the spectators and the shame of the owners!

Eta Pauptit races most of her Afghans and at one time would not show them in the ring unless they had proved themselves capable of winning races on the track.

With so much mixed Afghan breeding today in all parts of the world, and with a nation's basic stock being mixed with recent American blood, and in turn mixed with dogs from neighbouring places, it is difficult if not impossible to pinpoint 'type' in different countries. I think the Dutch are nearer than anyone to an individual type because of the work done by Miss Pauptit. And I must say she has plenty of devotees. There is now an International magazine, reguarly published, containing world-wide news of stock from the Oranje Manege kennels. Miss Pauptit took great pains to sell her stock to people who would consult her as to its eventual breeding and consequently the Oranje Manege strain has remained one of the purest in the world.

In some countries it is quite easy to make an Afghan into a Champion, in others very difficult. In France the title 'French Champion' can only be given at the Paris International show and, as a result, there is only one French Champion dog and bitch made up each year. In England it is tough making up a Champion. Remember you need three different shows and three different judges to gain your three Certificates — but you will find up to 400 dogs and bitches chasing the two Certificates at each show. And yet, having judged dozens of shows and a couple of thousand Afghans so far, I must admit I find it strange to see in a show ring dogs that in my opinion are not Champions even though they bear that title. And from what I hear it is the same the world over.

In some countries it is possible to make an Afghan into a

Champion without ever competing with another Afghan. In theory this could happen in many places. It certainly has happened in Australia and as a result other countries have regarded the Australian title as a cheap one. This has been grossly unfair to Australian breeders who have worked hard over the years to improve their stock. But the so called 'Bush' shows in Australia have Afghan classes with very few specimens competing. On the other hand at the big 'Royal' shows in Brisbane, Sydney, Melbourne and Adelaide, the figures show well over 100 Afghans trying for top honours.

There are Afghan Hound Clubs in nearly all the countries that have Afghans but naturally numbers vary considerably. In some cases there is just one Club but America has thirty five! One common factor is that they all work hard to improve the breed in all its aspects. Through these clubs Afghan enthusiasts wherever they may be are able to keep in touch with show news, breeding programmes, recent imports and exports and world-wide news about the breed.

It is interesting that in every country one or two breeders are always to the fore. In Holland it is Eta Pauptit, in Spain it is Cynthia Madigan, in Belgium it is Madame Fosse, in Ireland Bob Margrain. The list is endless. Over the years I have corresponded with His Highness the Maharaja of Baria whose kennel is dominant in India. He is quite a colourful figure by all accounts and, although we have never met, we tend to greet each other as old friends in writing. In the early 1970s I sold the Maharaja a puppy that he regards as his favourite and it is a Palace pet as well as being a Champion. His kennel is based on Eileen Snelling's famous 'Khorrassans' from England. In the 1920s many Afghans – some stolen – were imprted into India but this trade seems to have stopped altogether now.

To end this Chapter on the breed world-wide I must mention the situation now in Afghanistan. This country has never welcomed foreigners for any length of time, though visitors are tolerated. In this respect the Afghan native seems to be quite similar to the Afghan dog! From the stories returning travellers tell, it seems that there are no dog shows there and so the native breed is not exhibited. Afghans in captivity appear to be exclusive to the Royal family as in olden days. There are packs of Afghans in the wild and in a recent book I read of a visitor being invited by a local chieftain to go hunting for Afghans. When the Afghan dog is caught it is domesticated as much as possible and then put to work guarding and herding sheep. This herding instinct is an interesting characteristic. I once sold a puppy to a farmer in Cheshire who uses it as a sheep dog and it is working all the time on the farm, and this seems to be happening now in the Afghan's native country.

The dog is fairly rare in Afghanistan and when one does leave the country it is taken out very quietly because the Afghans still do not like the dogs leaving their homeland. There is a recent story of a visitor who smuggled two hounds out of Afghansistan covered in mud and unrecognisable — otherwise they could not have left.

From all accounts the native Afghan dogs still have a fierce temper and are very sparse in coat. No one in recent years has brought a 'show' specimen out of the country and yet my own feeling is that the breed in Europe would be improved by the careful selection of an Afghan from Afghanistan. Several have made their way to the West in recent times, but there is no way of registering them with the official Kennel Clubs, who are reluctant to recognise a dog unless its parentage can be properly ascertained.

So, ironically, it is impossible for the native Afghan to prove his potential worth.

A gold and a black and tan

Health

The Afghan Hound is an exeptionally healthy breed and has no dominant hereditary illnesses or diseases, though in recent years two diseases have been reported: hip dysplasia and juvenile cataract. Unfortunately both these can be traced back to American dogs and the diseases there were reported a good ten years before they became apparent in Europe. I wrote in my weekly column in *Dog World* in 1964 that 'British Afghans are fortunate not to be afflicted by hip dysplasia and juvenile cataract', and my comments were not challenged at that time by any breeder in Britain.

I have known many Afghans go through a fourteen and fifteen year life span without ever receiving veterinary attention apart from their vaccination, and so most of the symptoms and illnesses listed here will probably never affect your Afghans.

Anaemia Symptoms might be white gums and the dog may be near collapse. This is an iron deficiency and feeding quantities of cooked liver will improve the situation but this could scour the dog. Get quick veterinary aid.

Arthritis Old dogs suffer from this and veterinary attention can help a great deal nowadays. The dog may cry when getting out of his bed and may be in obvious pain when moving. Aspirin relieves the pain a little. Keep the Afghan warm and dry at all times.

Bad Breath The cause can be decayed and dirty teeth, mouth ulcers, worms, digestive troubles or kidney disease. A vet's job really, but charcoal biscuits help some digestive problems and chlorophyll tablets help bad breath.

Broken bones If you suspect a broken bone move the dog as little as possible and do take care not to get bitten. Immediate attention by the vet is needed.

Car sickness This can take the form of vomiting or heavy drooling. Try to avoid feeding the dog for eight hours before a long car journey. Travel pills may help but it is a good idea to get your puppy Afghan used to travelling in a car. Always carry a quantity of newspaper in the car in case of any accidents.

Collapse or fainting Call vet immediately. Remove the dog out of the hot sun into a darkened room. Make it comfortable on cushions or something similar. Pull the tongue out of the mouth to assist with breathing and dampen the mouth with water. When the dog comes round it can be very distressed so calm it by talking and stroking.

Coughing Kennel cough is quite serious and needs veterinary attention as it can exhaust a dog. Check that there is no obstruction in the throat and offer the dog a small bowl of milk. If the cough persists it is a vet's job.

Diarrhoea Very often caused by a change of diet and increased roughage in the food might improve the condition. If it persists check with the vet taking a sample of faeces. If there is blood in the motion get veterinary advice immediately.

Distemper Symptoms are a discharge from the eyes and nose, listlessness, off food, vomiting. Needs veterinary treatment immediately but do not take the dog to the vet's surgery. The dog *can* recover but distemper often proves fatal. Vaccination is the *only* safeguard. Ignore any advice about herbal medicine warding off the disease. Without vaccination this killer disease will almost certainly affect your dog.

Eating filth and faeces Probably a vitamin deficiency so feed the recommended dose of Canoval tablets. Do stop the dog doing this as it can become a habit.

Eye discharge Might be dust or dirt in the eye – just as well to check with the vet for eye drops or bathing solution.

False pregnancy This is fairly common in Afghans and becomes apparent about eight weeks after a bitch is in season. The bitch can be quite distressed and whines. The nipples sometimes enlarge and she fills with milk. Many novices are worried that the bitch has been accidentally mated because the symptoms are so much like a real pregnancy. False pregnancies are a nuisance and, although it is rare, I have known a bitch go right through the stages of labour – contractions and all. Keep the bitch active to take her mind off her condition, but if the false pregnancy becomes unbearable to you or the bitch you can get veterinary advice. Watch out for signs of milk hardening in the breast.

Fits Very distressing to see and the dog is very frightened when it comes out of a fit. You must get immediate veterinary advice. The dog is not aware of what is happening and you should place it comfortably in a darkened room.

Head shaking Examine ears to see if they need attention. If nothing can be seen, e.g. wax, sores, pus, it could be ear mites. Check with your vet for safety's sake.

Heart trouble This sometimes affects older dogs. Symptoms are panting hard after a walk. Modern research has helped tremendously and an affected dog can lead a fairly normal and active life to a good age. Requires veterinary attention, of course.

Hernia Many puppies have hernias and these never bother them through life. It can take the form of a large 'button' on the abdomen and rarely needs attention.

Kidney trouble Symptoms are constantly drinking from water bowl and frequent and sometimes uncontrollable evacuation of the bladder. Veterinary attention is required and your vet will want a sample of urine. Tablets can control very effectively.

Limping Examine paws for glass, cuts, tears, pieces of grit. Feel along the leg to see if the dog yelps. If the condition persists get vet's advice.

Mammary tumours Fairly common in Afghan bitches. They usually start with a series of hard buttons near the teats but do not appear to cause any distress to the bitch. I would not recommend surgery unless they get very large or burst. If this happens immediate veterinary attention is required.

Penis discharge Unusual in a healthy dog – check with vet.

Poor eater Vary the diet, check with vet who can prescribe a suitable tonic.

Rickets Fairly uncommon nowadays. This is the result of calcium deficiency, usually in rearing. Bone meal will assist the condition but checking with the vet is recommended. I have seen a very bad case of rickets improve 100% with proper treatment. Symptoms are a mis-shapen bone – particularly front legs – and slight 'bowing' of the front with elbows stuck right out.

Scratching Could be fleas or lice. Examine the roots of the coat and if there is any evidence of infestation get a bathing solution from the vet. The coat should be examined frequently for parasites which are easily picked up. Many remedies available from pet shops are not effective so I recommend vet's assistance.

Sores and cuts These need attention as soon as they are seen. Bathe with warm water and diluted antiseptic. Do not bother the vet with these unless they become inflamed.

Too fat Does your Afghan get enough exercise? Are you feeding too much? Cut out tit-bits and table scraps. Cut down on biscuits. Check with vet if the Afghan continues to be overweight. Can affect his heart or cause infertility.

Too thin Is the dog a poor eater? Check with vet.

Vaginal discharge Check with vet. Could be womb trouble but might be nothing at all.

Vomiting This can be a symptom for a number of things. It can be ignored unless it becomes regular or your Afghan is in obvious distress. Worms can be the cause but so can intestinal obstruction. Get vet's advice if worried.

Worms Worms are a nuisance from birth to old age. Modern worming techniques mean you can safely worm your Afghan regularly, and this is advisable. But do get the worming medicine from your vet as concoctions sold by pet shops are rarely effective. If worms are seen in the motions the infestation could be serious and if they are vomited the same can be said. Worms cause a dry and listless coat condition and sometimes the dog goes off its food.

Whining for no apparent reason Feel the body all over exerting gentle pressure to see if the pain can be located. Might be arthritis – but if the dog is continually distressed get veterinary attention.

Do remember that dogs which show any symptoms of illness should be kept away from other dogs; and dogs with any signs of disease or which have been in contact with any disease must never be taken to a dog show.

It sounds as though you will have an ever open purse and that your vet will retire a millionaire early in his career. But I must emphasise that you may never have to pay him a visit. Be guided by intuition but if any symptom is severe then take immediate action. It could be costly to ignore illness and disease. For timely treatment and advice the occasional vet's bill is a small price to pay for peace of mind.

READING LIST

Brearley and Barbaresi, *The Afghan Hound.* T.F.H publications. 1965.

Miller C. O. and E. M. Gilbert, *The Complete Afghan Hound* Howell Book House. 1965.

McDowell Lyon, *The Dog in Action.* Howell Book House. 1966

Hall, W. L., *The Afghan Hound.* Gifford. 1971.

Harrisson, C., *The Afghan Hound.* Popular Dogs Publications Ltd. 1974.

Harmer, Hilary, *Dogs and How to Breed Them.* John Gifford Ltd. 1974.

USEFUL ADDRESSES

The Kennel Club, 1 Clarges Street, Piccadilly, London W1Y 8AB, England.

The American Kennel Club, 51 Madison Avenue, New York, N.Y. 10010, USA.

There are many clubs catering for this breed and the addresses of these can be obtained from your Kennel Club.

DOG MAGAZINES

Pure Bred Dogs, American Kennel Gazette, published by the American Kennel Club.

Dog World, 22 New Street, Ashford, Kent, England.

Our Dogs, 5 Oxford Road Station Approach, Manchester 1, England.

Index

Distributors for
Bartholomew Pet Books

Australia

Book Trade : Tudor Distributors Pty. Limited, 14 Mars Road,
Lane Cove 2066, New South Wales, Australia

Canada

Pet Trade :   Burgham Sales Ltd., 558 McNicoll Avenue,
Willowdale (Toronto), Ontario, Canada M2H 2E1
Book Trade : Clarke Irwin and Company, Limited,
791 St. Clair Avenue W., Toronto, Canada M6C 1B8

New Zealand

Pet Trade :   Masterpet Products Limited,
7 Kaiwharawhara Road, Wellington, New Zealand
Book Trade : Whitcoulls Limited, Trade Department, Private Bag,
Auckland, Wellington, or Christchurch, New Zealand

South Africa

Book Trade : McGraw-Hill Book Company (S.A.) (Pty.) Limited,
P.O. Box 23423, Joubert Park, Johannesburg,
South Africa

U.S.A.

Pet Trade :   Pet Supply Imports Inc., P.O. Box 497, Chicago,
Illinois, U.S.A.
Book Trade : The Two Continents Publishing Group Limited,
30 East 42nd Street, New York, N.Y. 10017, U.S.A.